FULL
CIRCLE

FULL
CIRCLE

A Full Circle Love Story of Life and Death

SUSAN A RING

Los Angeles, California

FULL CIRCLE PRESS

FULL CIRCLE
Copyright @2020 by Susan A Ring.
All rights reserved.

Full Circle Press books may be purchased for other educational, business, or sales promotional use. For further information, please e-mail us at fullcirclepress01@gmail.com Los Angeles, California.

FIRST EDITION

Book Jacket, Pictures and Page Design:
Susan A Ring - Los Angeles, California

Library of Congress Cataloging-in-Publication Data
is available upon request.

ISBN 978-1-7336266-1-3

For all of the loves of my life

-With Love and Gratitude

Contents

A NOTE FROM THE AUTHOR

This book, *Full Circle* is my third memoir. All of my books can be read as standalones or read as a series of three. My first book is titled *The Unexpected Mother,* and the second is *When Hope Becomes Life.*

The first book was about my own extraordinary experiences as a surrogate mother and journeys through two surrogate experiences, and the second book was about my experience working with O Magazine during a photo shoot along with three more surrogacy journeys.

It's important to note that I was a surrogate mother and gave birth to eight surrogate babies, two singletons and three sets of twins for five different families throughout an entire decade of my life, all of my forties. Each surrogacy endeavor is called a *journey.* Each of my five journeys as a surrogate mother were different and unique.

My books are full of real-life drama in my life at the time, and contain a lot of things people are uncomfortable talking about. I believe truth is important in nonfiction stories and I have written all of my memoirs based on the simple foundation of truth.

One thing is for sure, I would not be writing books at all if it wasn't for the NDE (Near Death Experience) I had the day my daughter was born in July, 2013. My NDE has given me the most realistic pair of glasses I've ever looked through to see the world around me. I see it now so differently than I ever have before. I tell my truth the way it is, and try not to hide who I am, which I acknowledge I've done in my past books. I've finally learned there is so little time in life that there's no use in trying to be someone else.

Life is short, and meant to be fully lived.

The title of my third book, *Full Circle,* was inspired by my Near-Death Experience (NDE) and all the circles in life, the never-ending circle of life in nature and the cosmos. I've been fortunate to have experienced a well-lived life *full circle* many times in my life – and most fully the day I died giving birth to my daughter.

While my first book, *The Unexpected Mother,* covers my first two surrogacy journeys and was on television many times, including PBS's *Bloodlines,* Dr. Oz, and Dr. Phil with various other news stations and in magazines, including O, The Oprah Magazine (Dec, 2003), O's Top Ten Anniversary Special (May, 2010), and People Magazine (March 2016), along with international magazines, none told the entire story.

In writing this book I relied on my notes, personal journals, many paper napkins, consultations with people who appear in the book, and calling up my own memories of these events. I have changed the names of most individuals in this book and, in some cases, modified identifying details to preserve anonymity. There are no composite characters or events in this book.

All of the following medical and technical information *during* my Near-Death Experience was told to me by my husband, Paul, and the doctors involved, or taken directly and quoted out of my medical records. The Near-Death was experienced and written by myself, Susan A Ring.

INSPIRATION

Carl Sagan was born in 1934 and died in 1996. He inspired me throughout the writing of this book. He was an American astronomer, cosmologist, astrophysicist, astrobiologist, author, science popularizer, and science communicator in astronomy and other natural sciences. He is best known for his work as a science popularizer and communicator.

He was famous for a quote he made upon signing out of his television show every night. He said, "We are all star stuff. We are a way for the cosmos to know itself." He explained further by saying, "The nitrogen in our DNA, the calcium in our teeth, the iron in our blood, the carbon in our apple pies were made in the interiors of collapsing stars. We are made of star stuff."

My NDE (Near Death Experience) aligned with a lot of what Carl Sagan talked about in the COSMOS television program in the 70s and what he passionately explained to so many people long ago.

After much research on the topic of NDEs and reading a lot of stories online and in books, I was amazed at how NDEs showed so many similarities, told by so many individuals. Something I know for sure is there are way too many NDE stories out there that are too similar for near death experiences not to be true. The stories all connect in various ways and are way too important not to pay attention to.

I'm no neurosurgeon, or celebrity, nor am I a rocket scientist to persuade you to believe what I say is true. What I am is an everyday person and mother, moved so much by my NDE that I had to write about it and share it with the world. It's part of what happens after you experience something so profound, you're driven to share it.

There is so much about NDEs that we don't understand to date, and may never understand but the similarities are overwhelming. NDEs delve into topics of the unknown about consciousness and a lot of other scientific things that scientists and the medical world cannot measure, and therefore many believe the unmeasured does not exist, until they experience it for themselves.

My story believes human consciousness is as real as we are living on this earth.

PART ONE

BEFORE

"Find what you love and let it kill you." – Charles Bukowski

"Sign of the Times" – song by Harry Styles. (Lyrics are about a mother losing her life during childbirth.)

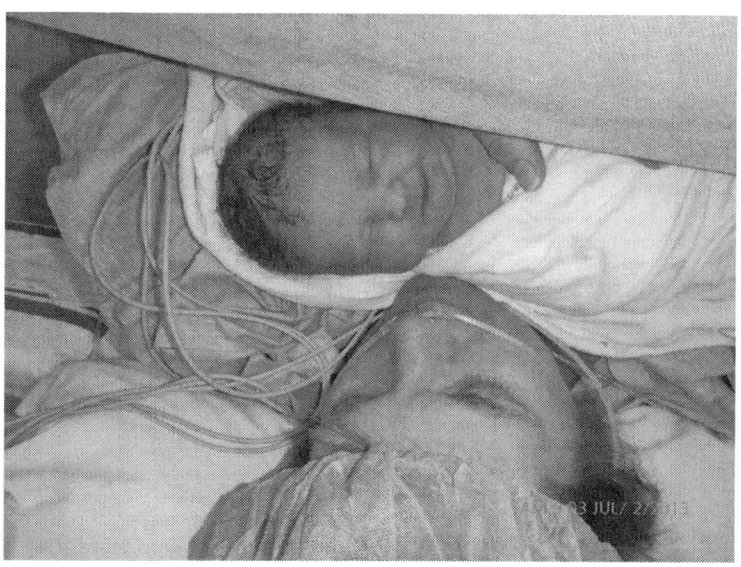

Chapter One

I awoke to the stirring of life in my womb. Emergence was inevitable and today was the day my daughter would be born, but I had no idea this would be the day I would die.

My abdomen slowly tightened hard with life emerging just below nine layers of skin inside the amniotic sac. I contracted all of my pelvic muscles to start labor pain. I squished my face up tight in pain at the peak of the contraction and then let it go. Right away I remembered the strength of contractions that comes with birth. My senses, especially my sense of smell was so heightened to the point that I could even smell the paint on the walls, the glue between the wooden slats on the floor. I knew the contractions would keep coming no matter what I did. I then remembered the most important thing in childbirth: to keep breathing. Deeply. Deeply, steadily, breathe.

I reflected on all of the past pain of childbirth, all of my seven birth experiences, remembering Mother Nature has a way of giving you just a little bit of amnesia after each birth, but when you start to go through it again, the memories of childbirth pain come back full force.

I always concentrated on the new life afterward, but this time, like the two first times, it was my child. Contractions catch all of your awareness and you know what you're in for, and there is no turning back. Now was the time I had to bring it to the table and be brave and strong. It reminded me of the natural contracting and expanding of the universe. I breathed deeply in, then out.

I reached my arm over to Paul, my husband, in bed and touched his arm gently.

"It's time, honey," I said to my new husband. We'd been married almost two years and it still felt wonderfully new. After waiting almost fifty years, I found this man.

"What!? Oh my God, are you okay?" he said, rising into a quick sitting position with me from a sound sleep. He placed his hand lovingly on my shoulder and looked deeply into my eyes to assess the situation.

"I'm having contractions. It's weird though, because my water broke first with all my other pregnancies. I don't feel any fluid between my legs so I don't think my water has broken," I wondered, and moved over in bed. "No, it hasn't broken yet," I said, sure of myself.

It was July, and I was a week away from my due date. I sat all the way up, put my hand on my large pregnant belly, and took in another deep breath. Paul was still watching me.

"Okay, let's be calm, and we'll get going to the hospital," Paul said, rising from bed. "I'll call into work and let them know I won't be in." He was amazingly calm and reached over for his phone. He worked for a huge company as a chemical engineer. Our daughter, still inside my womb, was his first child.

This would be the eleventh child I'd given birth to, so I wasn't worried about childbirth. I knew what would happen and how it would happen. I was confident every single time and never had a problem with any of the birth experiences.

"Don't worry, hun, I'm fine," I said. "I don't think I'm in labor but I can't be sure. I hate not being sure though." Something felt off but I had no idea what. It was truly odd to wake up so uncertain and confused about it.

I birthed two boys of my own from a prior marriage. After my divorce I became a single mother and raised my boys, Brian and Steven, now grown and off on their own.

While my sons were young, I answered a personal calling to become a surrogate mother and gave birth to eight babies for five different families. My birth history went like this: Son (mine), son (mine), surrogate boy, surrogate twins, surrogate - twins, surrogate boy, surrogate twins, and this time, in a new marriage, it was our own, a daughter.

Intuition, even if I didn't know it at the time, always guided me to where I needed to go. I relied heavily on it, even though I didn't listen to it some of the time. I was still learning to take it all in and believe in the magic of it all.

I walked into the kitchen to get something cold to drink thinking about what I was going to wear to the hospital. Maternity clothes no doubt.

I remembered one of the first times Paul and I got away for the weekend when we were first dating. We'd gone to Vegas to see Rugby, my first time. When I was dressing myself the morning of the game, I grabbed a pair of jeans thrown over the chair and put them on. They felt different, not quite like my own jeans. I looked down at what I thought were my jeans and saw that I had put Paul's jeans on, and they fit! We had a great laugh about that time.

I looked over by the window sill when I saw a flash of red. My eyes focused down on the red, and sitting outside on the window sill was a red cardinal perched and ready to fly if I moved or disturbed him in any way. He hesitated and looked at me, cocking his head from one side to another. I stared at him and took in his beauty, the way the black ring came around the bill locking together, blended in with the soft and bold-red wings. He was curious. I was curious.

I'm not a superstitious person but I'd seen him numerous times in the last few days. He'd always stop and watch me at the window sill. I felt another tightening of my whole abdomen with what felt like a Braxton Hicks contraction. It tightened to the max and my tummy was as hard as a rock. After it relaxed, I was still standing in the same place and the cardinal was still at the window. I waited a minute before I called for Paul. When I heard him in the hallway, I rested my arm on my huge tummy.

"Honey, have you seen the red cardinal at the window sill in the kitchen?" I asked.

"No, no I haven't," he said curiously. "Why?"

"I've been seeing one here for the last few days, like four, five, maybe six times."

He didn't comment or seem to give it another thought because we were headed out the door, needing to be on our way to the hospital. I reached for my cold water, Paul came rounding the corner to the kitchen, and the red cardinal flew away.

All the way to the hospital I couldn't get my mind off the red cardinal. I thought I remembered reading that they were highly regarded as spiritual messengers in some cultures but I didn't know that to be a fact. I knew it might just be a hope or an idea and that cultures and even religions had their own beliefs of what cardinals represented. I'd read that Cardinals in the Catholic Church hierarchy wear the deep red robes to signify the presence of power and spirit.

The one that resonated with me most was the article I read that suggested people who see cardinals repeatedly might have just lost a loved one. I thought of my mom; it had been almost five years since she passed away. It'd be just like her to come late, or anytime she wanted. I smiled.

We made it well within time to the largest hospital in the South Bay just off the coast of southern California. It was a Catholic hospital but we were not Catholic. It just happened to be the best hospital around so we decided to go with it.

I remember walking up to the front of the building with

Paul and him admiring all of the statues of marble saints and angels, and then all of the beautiful and colorful artwork throughout the hospital.

In the labor and delivery emergency room, they hooked me up to the monitors to track my contractions. The second they hooked me up I heard the sound of galloping horses. I loved that sound. I sat back and listened to our daughter's heartbeat. It calmed me.

I was monitored for a few hours in the early morning because my contractions had subsided and slowed down. My amniotic water was still in place. It hadn't broken. I thought maybe this wasn't the day. It didn't feel like our daughter's birthday. Maybe I could go home.

Dr. Chen, my OBGYN came into the room. "What do think you guys? Today can be the day because the holiday is coming up and there will be less people in the hospital then to help out," he said, waiting for the go ahead.

I thought about this, and how it would be practical and more convenient for him and others in the hospital. I then realized today might be the day our daughter would be born.

"You can pick the time," he said. It was now clear he wanted to move as soon as possible.

Paul looked at me for guidance, waiting for an answer, and I looked to him for some stability with how I was feeling, but I didn't really even know how I was feeling. I wasn't sure what to say to him. I was hesitant because all the other times I had felt clear, and confident.

Perhaps the reason for my uncertainty was because this was my first delivery with Dr. Chen, and questions kept popping up in my head. Paul and I had discussed if often, and we decided to stay with Dr. Chen because it was close to home and he had twenty-five years of wisdom as an experienced OBGYN.

I must have looked perplexed and concerned because in truth I wasn't so sure this was the day. Something felt off. Things weren't going like they did with all the other births. I knew I wouldn't have the option for a regular labor and delivery procedure because of the risk with my age (my OBNGYN had said this from a definitive medical point of view) and because I've had multiple C-sections. My OBGYN ordered a C-section which meant we would have the first choice of an operating room due to high risk. In the past I always wanted to do natural childbirth, I now didn't fight it because I had a certain sense of confidence with doctor and wanted what was best for both of us and the safety of my baby.

"Okay. So today is the day." I said this even while not believing a word of it.

The doctors and nurses started prepping everything while we waited to be moved to the operating room. Less than an hour later we were in the surgical room. Paul was suited up in all the surgical garb and mask so he could be in the room with us. It was his first birth experience. I thought about all the other births I'd had and couldn't wait to see his face the moment he saw his daughter born. After a few births, I'd learned to wait for the moment. The moment the parents see their baby being born and their faces light up with the purest, fullest human joy and awe at the miracle of birth. They see what they've been waiting for all this time: Their child. A child they can love, hold, and watch grow up. These moments have held the purest, most unabashed expressions of joy and happiness I've ever experienced and felt in my lifetime.

All the nurses and doctors moved into their positions for the birth.

"Okay, you ready, honey?" Paul asked.

"Think so," I offered unsteadily.

Dr. Chen said, "Ready to meet your daughter?"

We both nodded.

He made the first cut nine layers deep into my body. I envisioned blood seeping out of yet another scar on my abdomen. It's something that can never be undone. It's with you for the rest of your life. A warrior war scar to remind you of birth.

The blue curtain used for C-sections dividing us was a nuisance, but I understood the need for it. I've been told the other side of the blue curtain is for people who can stomach the insides of people, like a doctor.

Once the cut was made, Paul was a bit hesitant about looking at my insides, having never seen a live surgery, but peeked over a few times to satisfy his curiosity.

The moment Dr. Chen made that incision it felt like my life was over. It always felt disconcerting to know during a C-section that they were cutting my abdomen wide open. Every time I've had a C-section (I had three prior to this one) it felt like my life was over. I know it's silly, irrational, but my fear was real, visceral. I'd always been against C-sections, and wanted to do all-natural births. But it just didn't work out that way for me after a certain point.

After four natural births years earlier, I finally had to have a C-section. At that time, I wasn't made aware that once I had a C-section I would then *always* have to have a C-section for all subsequent births, due to potential problems for me and weakening of the muscular uterine walls. The explanation was somewhat complicated at the first C-section but it came down to the strong likelihood there *might be* weight issues for the babies due to the difference in birth weights when I carried twins.

C-sections are invasive and weakens everything within a woman's body. There is nothing light or easy about them. With my earlier births I had an OBGYN who liked doing C-sections and boasted about his celebrity patients. I wasn't moved by this and didn't want one. My intuition told me and I believed bottom line that he was uncomfortable delivering twins naturally.

There was nothing I could do in that situation. My hands were tied. The OBGYN maintained it was because of the weight of the babies, but he couldn't prove it except through ultrasound, which is almost always off. I think we would have been fine with a natural labor, but I couldn't push it because *what if?* It was the *what-ifs,* and I believe a third-party liability for the OBGYN, that resulted in the C-section.

What if something happened during the natural birth? What if I was wrong? As a surrogate mother, I wasn't willing to gamble with my intended parents' babies so I went along with the doctor's medical suggestion to have my first C-section – and hated every minute of it. I had no other choice but to go with the medical decision of the doctor with the worried intended parents standing by.

Dr. Chen proceeded to help our daughter come into the world, to do the thing he'd done so many times in his twenty-five years of delivering babies. It was his job to get her out of my womb safely and to breathe in air for the first time into her brand new fully-formed baby lungs.

With his mask over his mouth and surgical cap covering his dark hair, I noticed his eyebrows furrow and that he looked somewhat perplexed. It seemed he was having trouble getting our daughter out of my womb. He pulled my body from one side to the other, and tugged and worked to pull her from my womb. *Popping* sounds were made each time Dr. Chen pulled my body to get her out. It sounded like popping bubble wrap each time he pulled. I started to shiver and couldn't get warm. I looked up at the anesthesiologist standing by my side.

"What are those popping sounds, doctor?" He looked at me, taking in what I said but didn't have an answer. "I never heard them during the three other C-sections I've had?" I questioned, hoping anyone around could hear me.

It was more than loud enough to notice. Did anyone notice?

As Dr. Chen maneuvered our child from my womb, the popping continued.

I looked up at the anesthesiologist again and he looked over at Dr. Chen.

"She said she hasn't heard popping sounds before during a C-section, and she's concerned," he said to both Dr. Chen and his partner.

"Okay," Dr. Chen said looking over at his colleague assisting him with the birth. Neither could find a reason nor any problems during the procedure.

The story of my life, I thought. Telling a man that I have a concern about my own body and him dismissing it for some reason or another. Or, I had to look at the troubling possibility that maybe he just didn't know what it was.

I weakly moved to lift my head and whispered to Paul, "This isn't normal, this popping sound."

At that moment, our attention was immediately pointed to the birth of our daughter. She was being pulled from my body. The doctor lifted her up so I could get a quick peek before he handed her to the nurse close by. She was perfect. There was a tad bit of crimson-brownish hair, and squeezed up eyes like she'd been sleeping and was awakened from a dream. She let out a little gasp and got a mouthful of air, and then her little cries of disturbance worked into big cries filling the room. She found her lungs.

I scanned her from a distance to make sure she had all her little fingers and toes then searched for any birthmarks that would make her unique. I realized Paul was there to keep watch over her, and the nurses went to their duties to measure her and clean her up.

"7 pounds, 14 ounces, 20 inches. She's perfect," Paul said with watery eyes and tears rolling down his cheeks. Paul kept a keen eye on her as the nurses continued about their work and Dr. Chen was getting me ready to be stitched up.

Our girl came from there to here, crossing over that invisible divide, the liminal space we can't see or measure, magical space that separates us from life and death.

I again caught sight of her sweet head of hair alive with that reddish-brown hue, and cried happy tears immediately at the sight. The experience of birth, of creating and growing a human being and assisting God in a miracle. Tears streamed down the sides of my face and onto the table I was lying on.

Paul looked on at both of us, never knowing where to place his gaze. On me, on her, then back and forth again and again. I smiled proudly.

The miracle of childbirth never got old for me. I never got the message I was done giving birth or having more children. Perhaps it is why I wanted to be a mother and surrogate mother so many times. Maybe it's because I loved being able to go and lightly touch the invisible divide whenever I welcomed a new life into the world.

I've always loved being pregnant. In fact, I loved it so much that pregnancy felt better for me than not being pregnant. The moments after birth were always the most phenomenal moments I've experienced in my life, until I experienced my own death.

The last memory before my NDE journey was watching my dear husband Paul, the love of my life (whom I had met just two and a half years before at the age of forty-nine) become a father. The man who taught me how to be a partner in life was a new daddy. He cradled our daughter's sweetness in his arms like a pro; the profound richness of his first child and my eleventh.

As a single mother for eleven years to two remarkable boys (from my first marriage), Brian and Steven, now in their twenties, I had waited a long time to find love again. I was a new wife and a new mother again, and very lucky to say I now had my second family.

While I was a single mother, and all through my forties, I'd also been a surrogate mother to eight children for five different families.

Thoughts raced through my mind about how beautiful life was, how grateful I had been to have good and healthy pregnancies. Every. Single. One. "Textbook pregnancies," my other OBGYN whom I'd used multiple times proudly said about my pregnancy history.

I took in every precious moment when the nurse handed

our daughter to her proud daddy. He gazed upon her, studying every inch of her face. He lifted her hand up and looked at her fingers, then opened the blanket she was wrapped in and glanced down at her legs then her toes. He took the blanket and wrapped her back up, bringing her to the crook of his neck to admire her. Paul saw me watching him and walked over to me, his arms full of life.

When Dr. Chen finished up with me post-labor, Paul brought our freshly wrapped daughter to my head. I gave her a little nuzzle as tears fell down the sides of my cheeks to my ears and off my head and into my hair beneath the surgical cap.

"Welcome to the world, beautiful daughter," I whispered to her and lightly kissed the top of her head with my dry lips.

I immediately thought of my beautiful mother who told me upon her deathbed that this daughter would come into my life. She said, "You will have a daughter, Susan."

My mother had made a little white lacy eyelet dress she wanted me to have for my daughter. In that moment she was as serious as I ever saw her.

I honestly thought my mother was delirious. I was forty-eight, a single mother of two, pregnant with my third set of twins as a surrogate mother and had absolutely no potential boyfriends. After 27,948 dates I wasn't getting any closer to finding someone I would go out with twice, let alone have another child of my own with. I definitely wasn't getting any younger either. And yet, now, here was this daughter my mother predicted, and I was a new mom again.

"Keep the dress," she had said with great insistence. "You'll need it." I smiled, and nodded in agreement. I held her close knowing every second of my mother's life mattered at that moment, in the latter days of her life. The doctors told us that she was ready for hospice and was in an active state of dying. She passed away just a few days later.

I always thought grief was kind of strange. People always want you to *let go, have closure, or move on with* a loved one, or just *get over* the death of someone because it makes them uncomfortable.

My mom's death was a complete surprise, as I learned lung cancer can be, when she went to the emergency room for a non-stop cough, and was dead sixteen days later. I was beyond shocked and grief hit me hard. Sometimes you feel too much during grief, and other times nothing at all. And just when grief eases up, it appears again all consuming and out of nowhere feeling like the weight of many worlds.

My memories blur sometimes of the past with my mother. I usually remember the sayings she used to say, or mother/daughter moments we shared together. I remembered mom, my aunt and me stuffing as many grapes as we could into our mouths and laughing at the sight of each other at the kitchen table at my grandmother and grandfather's house. My mom taught me how to throw cooked spaghetti up against the wall to see if it was done. If it stuck, it was done. If it fell down it wasn't done.

I knew one day I'd lose her, but not at that time. I wasn't ready. She was my *mother*, she gave me life and loved me no matter what. No one loved me like she did.

Over time I learned a new way to do grief. I decided to carry her memory with me every day for the rest of my life. You don't *get over*, or *let go* of love like that. I never stopped thinking about and carrying my mother with me through and after the grieving process. Sometimes I still grieve, but in different ways. I still bring her into the present sometimes even though she left this world in January of 2008. She's indeed here, with me, anytime I think of her. In the last year of her life she would often say to me, "I'll always be right here on your shoulder whenever you need me," and pat my shoulder to intensify her meaning.

The last time I saw my mother alive my siblings and I were saying goodnight to her. She was in a temporary home waiting for a room with hospice. She was in her bed propped up, telling all of us kids she loved us, one at a time. I had to fly back home to southern California for work and planned on seeing her the following weekend.

She made it to Wednesday. She left me with an "I love you." A meaningful goodbye: *I love you.* The difference was she'd usually just say "love you" so casually at the end of our phone conversations. But this time, she said it with depth, meaning and finality. I can still hear it in a whisper.

But, how did she know this would happen? How did she know I would have a daughter that it would actually happen? I wondered.

Before Paul and I decided to start a family together, we'd looked at adoption and other ways to parent and ran into barriers of discrimination we weren't expecting. *Too old* came up often so nothing came easier for us, mostly me, than to do it ourselves via IVF – In Vitro Fertilization.

Paul didn't have children of his own before I met him. If we went this route, he could be expecting his first biological child.

"It doesn't matter to me if we adopt or whatever, I'd just like to parent with you." Paul said.

By the time we found our way through all the forms and endless paperwork of other options, we decided on IVF. With my history in the IVF world, I'd been through enough IVF cycles that I knew the ins and outs of the procedures and which medical doctors to go to. We scraped together all of our funds to do IVF and created beautiful embryos. They were gorgeous full circle embryos, just like the moon or the earth. Perfect spheres of life that would come up every time we tried, but none would work due to my age.

My IVF doctor had hope for me and we tried with my own eggs five times. The IVF doctor, Dr. Yanagi, comped us a cycle because he wanted me to be the world's oldest mother to conceive via IVF. The oldest woman at the time to be successful was forty-eight years old.

We would end up using donor eggs for our daughter. My dinosaur eggs would not work. It was hard accepting the fact that my eggs wouldn't work.

At the beginning of this pregnancy, the IVF doctor confirmed twins. We were so excited to have two on the way! Both embryos had taken and then the unexpected happened. I started to bleed heavily at eleven weeks pregnant. I thought for sure I'd lost both the babies, the whole pregnancy. It would be the first time I'd experienced a pregnancy loss after a confirmed pregnancy.

Upon my waking in the early morning hours with very heavy bleeding, Paul and I quickly made our way to the emergency department. The ultrasound technician knew the story and couldn't contain her excitement in waiting for the doctor to give us the results.

"There is still a heartbeat! Look!" she said to us as she pointed at the screen.

There was our girl, one lonely little heart beating away on the ultrasound screen. After a lot of blood loss, how was it that she was still here with us? The tech turned up the sound to the machine and we heard a thousand horses galloping with the quiet hum of the ultrasound machine. We were elated. We'd lost her twin but she was still with us. I was so sad about losing one, yet so happy that our little one was still there. It was so bittersweet for us.

Back in the operating room after about thirty or forty-five minutes, Dr. Chen finished up with me post labor and sewed me up tight after the C-section.

Our daughter stopped crying and started in with the new dialog of newborn squeaks. I really wanted to hold her but suddenly didn't trust myself. I questioned it in my mind, this pivotal moment in time, and I felt shaky even while I was lying down. Something wasn't right. I was unsteady, dizzy and lightheaded. I've passed out before so I knew the feeling of becoming unconscious. It scared me and it never happened when I was lying down.

"Baby, I can't hold her, I feel really weak, something is wrong with me," I said to Paul, feeling dizzy and confused. "I knew that popping sound I heard wasn't right, I just knew it." I was having trouble breathing and gasped between my words.

Paul looked over my way, and brought our daughter over to me gently placing her on the top of my chest so she couldn't fall, and she'd be in the security of my arms. Our girl was beautiful and wasn't named yet. We had a few names chosen but wanted to see her little face first.

Life was amazing and I was the luckiest mother on earth.

"There is blood in her urine," Dr. Chen's colleague said in surprised voice. I remember the look on her face of sheer disbelief, her intense dark eyes sending out an alert.

I looked up at her and she seemed frozen in time. There was only her surprised face. She looked over at Dr. Chen. We all exchanged shocked looks.

I knew "blood in her urine" was a sign I was bleeding internally.

The looks of surprise were on everyone's faces, especially the anesthesiologist. Those were looks that stop you dead in your tracks. What happened? What went wrong? Things seemed to be happening so fast, yet so slow. I felt fuzzy headed and became disoriented. The anesthesiologist stayed by my side and reached for controls on the other side of my body on the IV drip and rechecked all of his controls on the machine.

"Clear here, Dr. Chen," he said as Dr. Chen nodded. He turned some controls and motioned for Paul to come over to him. Paul walked up to listen to him.

"You'll need to take the baby," he said. Paul's eyes looked worried.

Paul reached over to take our daughter from my arms and looked hesitantly at the doctor.

"It's going to be okay," Paul said to me in a faint whisper.

I kissed her on the forehead, taking in her newborn baby smell. Paul kept looking at the doctors for reassurance. He waited for an answer from someone for what was going on. No one had answers.

It was almost like everyone was suspended, frozen in time until Dr. Chen said clearly and firmly, "we'll have to open her back up." He said this in a hurried way, like time mattered.

Suddenly we were flanked by new doctors and nurses hurriedly moving about the room then moving into panic mode. I'm not sure who said what during those critical moments, but one of them ushered Paul away to the side of the room up against the white tile wall while the doctors tried to stabilize me.

Paul grabbed at his face mask to try and breathe and hold our daughter. After trying to stabilize me, another nurse or doctor led Paul to the front door of the surgery room. Paul told me later that he noticed a pool of blood on the floor underneath my body before he left the surgery room.

I followed them with my eyes to the door, and saw Paul turn around to look at me through the square windows to the doors with our new bundle of joy. I can still see the blue-green eyes I fell in love with full of worry for me, an image that will always be in my mind somewhere between the folds.

I wasn't filled with panic, but knew I had to let go big here. The what ifs and maybe-it-will-kill-you came in. I let go of those thoughts and knew I had to trust. The doctors all knew what they were doing and my life was in their hands.

I sensed that I had a fraction of a second to say my goodbyes to the loves of my life, Paul, my sons Brian and Steven, and our newborn daughter along with my whole family.

I am the type of person who never said *goodbye*. I avoided it at all costs. I was the type of person who would say '*see you later*' always. But this particular time, I knew it was goodbye.

Saying goodbye to me implied that sometimes you must

heal emptiness, many injuries and wounds of the soul. I had an innate feeling to hold on all of my life, not let go. I worked so hard to get where I was. I wasn't ready to say goodbye.

But there was an invisible acceptance response pulling me to say goodbye, and it felt like I was not coming back to this world.

I trusted the knowing. In my mind I said, *I love you all, goodbye.*

My eyes closed.

I thought I was gone. It was like falling asleep. Was this unconsciousness? But why was I thinking and questioning? Why was I remembering every word I just said in my head? Why was my mind so active? Everything surrounding me was dark, like I was in the middle of the color black.

I assumed it to be the liminal space I often dreamed about, another realm, in-between worlds just like what might have been before— I had a vision of being in my mother's womb or another place fifty-two-years before in December of 1960, in Oceanside California before I was born.

Here I was, right after our daughter was born, my eleventh child, and becoming a new mother again that I was teetering in between two worlds, the beginning and the end, hers and mine, this life and the next. I'd slipped into that marvelous invisible divide and crossed over the thin membrane that I had danced upon so many times in my life, this invisible in-between.

And then what felt like a split-second later there was light, glorious life-giving light. It was dazzling, brilliant, and everywhere around me. The light was absorbed within my body and it lifted me up toward the sky. It had a magnetic pull so strong I moved upward without any resistance or hesitation. Consciously, I knew I was leaving the planet. I didn't look behind me because I knew wherever I was going was the place I needed to be.

I trusted completely. There was no question in my mind as to why or how. I never fully trusted in my life, but I did at this moment. I soared up, flying into the light with my hospital gown flowing behind me in the wind. It felt like I innately knew how to fly, like I did sometimes in my dreams. It felt like I'd been flying all of my life. I didn't have wings, but I was flying!

The light was so bright it made my eyes squint nearly shut. I could feel the light vibrating throughout my body with love. *The love was the light?* I wondered. What I knew for sure was it was a love stronger than anything I've ever felt. This love wasn't of this world.

I was on my way home.

Chapter Two

In Oceanside, California there was a cute little fire station on the corner of our neighborhood. My mother bought a house close to it for an unbelievably low amount back then and shared it with my biological father until he abandoned my mother, me and my two older siblings right after I was born. I didn't see him again until I was nineteen.

In my visits to the fire station, which was only a half a block away, I learned that if I climbed way up onto the fire engine where the firemen couldn't get to me without also climbing up, the firemen would bribe me with a quarter to get down. There weren't really paramedics then, but I remembered them as firemen. I was always over at the fire station when I wasn't riding my tricycle.

Growing up as a little girl in the sixties, the earliest memory I have of tempting danger was when I was four years old. My mother caught me and a little boy from down the street playing with matches in a large dry bush out in the front yard of our home, something I'm sure the firemen would certainly have frowned upon.

My mother caught me, and maybe my older sister told on me. My mother was angry. She decided to teach me a lesson about *how not to play with matches.*

"Susan Ann!" she'd yell. I knew what it meant when I heard her call me with my middle name, and I'd run really fast to try to get away from her.

Once she caught me, she would use chocolate to hold me. It always worked. My blurry memory revealed my mother holding me close, sitting in her lap while she was seated on the couch in the living room. She lit the head of a round, red-tipped match, blew it out and lifted it to the fresh pink skin of my forefinger. I fought and fought as I watched her lift the match to my finger, but she was stronger than I was. I knew what she was going to do, she was going to burn me with the match! I could feel her energy, her anger. I remember being shocked and mad at her for hurting me.

I'm not sure it taught me not to play with matches. I think it taught me how not to get caught the next time I decided to do something stupid.

Chapter Three

1966, I'M SIX

One beautiful early summer afternoon at my grandparent's house in Palo Alto my mother announced she would take all us kids to the pool where my grandfather had a membership. We all loved that pool at The Elk's Club. The pool was always clear blue and so inviting. We would stay for hours and hours. There was always someone to play with.

My mother was driving me, my sister and my cousins to the pool down the tree-lined streets of eucalyptus trees standing taller than any trees I'd ever seen. Swimming was an activity I lived for, and I loved to swim at that pool. I'd beg and beg to go anywhere that had water. The beach, feeding the ducks, but mostly the pool because it was more convenient for my mom, and we went more often during the summer.

On the car ride to the pool, I was directly behind my mother while we were all bouncing around in the back seat of the car. Back then no one used seatbelts as it wasn't the law yet. As I leaned on the front seat directly in back of my mother's head, she turned around and looked right at me, one inch from my face, and said with hot breath, "Do not go into the deep end. Do you hear me, Susan Ann?"

Apparently, she'd had trouble with me before going into the deep end before I knew how to swim. I nodded like I understood.

But just as soon as my mother put my bathing cap on for the first time since the pool opened that summer, I marched over to the new, white, and most tempting fifteen-foot diving board. It was fresh, shiny and new. I walked slowly up the stairs admiring the fresh paint. When I got to the top, it was windy. I proceeded to walk to the end of the wiggly diving board not knowing I might not be able to return to the stairs.

My little girl mind had second thoughts about being up there. Standing on the end of the wobbly board, I felt dizzy and couldn't keep my balance like I usually could. There was no going back. I'd fall for sure, maybe hit the concrete. I didn't know what to do but I knew I'd have to jump to get down. This all swam inside my head. There was only one option. I jumped into the windy air without hesitation, without fear. Freefall.

I remember my body smacking the surface of the water, and letting out a little cry for help. I fell deep into the water and went down, down, down. I opened my eyes and saw no one near me, just the distant legs of the kids and adults kicking and swimming in the pool. I flailed my arms underneath the deep blue of the pool trying to reach up to the bright sunlit top. It seemed so far away. The pool was huge. I tried to find something to push off of but I was in the middle and just floating. It was all going too slow, and didn't think I'd make it to the top fast enough to breathe. I didn't know what to do. I floated up some more and seemed to stop midway in the depths of the blue, and looking up saw the sparkly sunny top. I watched the bottom half of bodies in the water oblivious to what was happening to me. They blurred in and out. The water all around me.

All of a sudden, I felt someone grab and pull and tug my little girl body. It hurt as they grabbed me and pulled me up, up, up to the surface. Once we hit the hot cement, I cried wondering why it was so hard to breathe. My throat hurt. I couldn't breathe and gasped for air.

"You're lucky to be alive!" a man's voice exclaimed.

I've dreamt many times since then about the sound of the water as the lifeguard pulled me up to the surface. *Whooosh… Whooosh.* And the bubbles upon bubbles. When I woke up from the dream, I remembered the feeling of coming up from the bottom of the pool for that first breath.

The lifeguard pushed me to my side, and I started coughing up water. Hard coughs pushed up mucous. I remembered how everything seemed to hurt all over, especially my throat.

The first face I saw was my mother's. I've never in my life seen her so mad at me as she was that day. My mother screamed, "GodDAMN it, Susan Ann, I told you!!"

I was immediately grounded and afraid I wouldn't be able to swim for the whole day or maybe longer. My sister was elated that I made my mother so furious, and that I was in trouble. Again. My sister danced in a circle around me saying, "Susan caaaaan't swim! Susan caaaaan't swim!" And my mother let her taunt me. I sat on a thin towel feeling the hot concrete beneath my bottom for a very long time. It felt like forever. My throat hurt for hours.

My mother would retell that story to me many times as I grew up. She'd say to other people that she made a mad dash, running as fast as she could to the lifeguard to save me.

But in my eyes, my mother was never a runner. I'm pretty sure I'd never seen her run in all my life. But maybe she did that day.

She'd say over and over, "I watched Susan go up that ladder thinking she'd turn back, but she never did." I'm pretty sure she used a lot of loud GodDAMN -it's in every telling of the story, too.

I came so close to death that day as a young child, and I believe it instilled in me a wicked sense of recklessness, maybe even the adoption of a risky attitude of dancing with death. Looking back on my life, I did it all the time as a young person and then well into my adulthood.

Chapter Four

1967, I'M SEVEN

When I was a little girl, I collected rocks. Lots of rocks, smooth ones, rough ones, large ones, small smooth ones were my favorites. I'd take them and brush them up against my cheek to feel the surface up against my skin. Then there were the ones that I could put in my pocket and carry around with me. Those were my very favorite because I could carry Mother Nature around with me. I felt safe with my rocks.

I found most of them at the ranch where us kids would play while our parents sat and drank all day in a circle by the barn underneath a large tin roof. I had my first Coca-Cola at the ranch. I'll never forget that first refreshing sip. The ranch was huge. It had dirt roads that led into the ranch and up to a small house at the top of the hill. There were about six barns on acres and acres of sparse land. Rolling hills of land for kids to play and discover on. I believe my connection to rocks was that I knew, even then, it was of mother earth. The earth is made of rock from the tallest mountains to the floor of the deepest oceans

There were a lot of things for little girl adventurers like me to do at the ranch. I'd venture out looking for special things to collect. One day I found a badger's skeleton It was cool. I was a little afraid of it when I was told by my sister it was going to eat me. But then I learned not to be scared, and there was a sense of calm the ranch provided for me. Nature was on my side, always on my side. I felt her watching out for me when I was out there breathing, running, flying kites, living life to the fullest on a mountain side, and soaking up her brilliance. Even as a child, I knew it was something extraordinary to commune with nature.

Upon one treasure hunt, I was there looking for treasure. I remember the day well. I had on white Keds sneakers with no socks, shorts and a tank top. I spotted something shining from the sun. It beckoned me and I walked up slowly to it. It was wedged in the earth. I kept walking closer to it realizing it might have magical powers. I had an active imagination and this type of discovery just made my mind much more inquisitive.

It was so extra sparkly and part of it was just glistening in the hot sun. I creeped up and reached out with my hand to touch the rock. It was hot. As I picked it up my hand hurt from the heat and I accidentally dropped it onto another rock. It broke open like a treasure chest. I raised part of it to the sun and crystals glimmered in a million brilliant shiny angles with a blue sky in the background.

I'd found something special and it was magical! I was thrilled.

It was my magic rock full of quartz crystals and it was the most precious gift I'd ever found out in nature, and better than any toys I'd ever had. After I'd find new rocks, I'd put them on display in my house on a table in the washroom all clearly labeled. I'm sure it drove my mother crazy because she liked keeping a clean house and dirty rocks on top of a table were not her idea of a clean kept house. I often couldn't find the rocks after I placed them up on that table. Sometimes I'd get a few days to admire them and other times my mother found them first. I learned to put them in a box under my bed or keep them under my pillow. I always had my special magic rock by my bed where I slept. I kept on with this way into my adult life too, collecting rocks. If I saw one catching my attention when I was out in nature, I still pick it up and put it in my pocket and put it in a collection I have in glass vases.

My mother had remarried when I was young and moved all of us to the valley of Oceanside. My life with a new stepfather was anything but normal, but I survived. He was mean to the bone, illogical, and scary. To ensure my survival, I'd leave the house early in the morning every day and not come back until the street lights were on.

After rock collecting or playing tag, my friends and I would meet at San Luis Rey Elementary school every day. We'd swing for hours on several chained swings and go as high as the swing would let us, far beyond the actual bar holding it together at the top. The chains of the swing were heavy-duty but made a high squeaky pitch as they moved back and forth from the moving round bar at the top.

When we'd get as far up as they could go, we'd jump out of the swing at that highest point and go flying through the air trying to beat each other's records by marking our place where we landed in the sand. We'd all root for each other, "Go higher, come on, go higher!" we'd scream to each other.

I often won and remember to this day the feeling of my arms and legs flailing and hurtling with force through the air, always coming down and hitting the ground with incredible strength. The higher I went the deeper the mark I made in the sand when I landed.

Now I admire that I was so carefree to fly through the air like I did with absolutely no fear of being hurt. Was it smart? Probably not, but we were kids.

When we got bored with the swing, we'd put a sweater on a jungle gym bar to swing around it with our legs fast, faster, the fastest we could go. Once I fell off the bar onto my back because I was going so fast because of the sweater tied to it. I fell and hit the dirt ground hard and blacked out. When I came to, I looked up to see the not-so-white sweater still tied around the bar.

The fall knocked the wind and living shit out of me. I couldn't get a clean breath and laid gasping for air on the dirt ground, taking in nothing but more dirt. I watched my surprised friends' faces as they stood huddled around me from up above. "That was so cool, do it again!" they said.

Surely, right that moment I remembered feeling as though I was dead, or would die right there in front of all of them wheezing and waiting for air to enter my mouth again. There on the ground, I was still wondering what the hell happened and in awe of how it happened so fast. It seemed to have taken a long time before I could get up again.

Later that same year right before I turned seven, I was playing in a creek full of dirty water with my friends. We were throwing wood 2x4s over the water and walking across on the boards. We'd done it all the time so it was nothing new. It was fun to find different things to throw over and walk across the creek on.

That particular day it was sunny and we were seeing who could do the best tricks as we walked across the boards where the school buses met to take the older kids to school. I decided to hop half way on the 2x4 in the middle where there was a visible split in the wood. As I hopped mid-way the board gave and my right ankle broke through into the water. I pulled my foot out of the water and saw blood. The blood gushed out and was making me dizzy. I looked over to where I fell near the splintered 2x4, and saw the broken bottom of an old green thick glass Gallo wine bottle sticking two inches up waiting to pierce the skin of careless kids.

It effortlessly pierced my skin, going deep with its sharp thick jagged green edge.

Blood continued to gush. It was clear to me no Band-Aid was going to fix this. The gash was about three inches long and my foot looked like it was hanging from the bone. The blood was coming out so fast I didn't know how I was going to get home a block away.

I yelled to my friends, "Go quick, go get my mom! I can't walk!" I started to get scared.

Mom came running out of the house with her red lipstick on and found me lying down in the middle of the street. I wasn't able to make it to the curb. She looked whiter than a ghost after she saw me and quickly wrapped my ankle. Seconds later the towel was filled with blood. Writing this now, I can still see the bloody towel, and feel the trauma and numbness of the deep cut.

Mom yelled at one of my friends, "GO! Get more towels in the house. All of them!" We were still all in the middle of the street, and more friends had gathered to see my blood. She wrapped and wrapped it, and I felt sleepier. She didn't have a car that particular day so she summoned the lady across the street and asked her if she'd take us to the doctor's office immediately. The lady was dumbfounded and almost fainted at the sight of all the blood. She drove us to the medical center on Cassidy Street.

"Just drive faster please!" my mom begged. They put me in the back of the station wagon because of all the blood. She'd glance at me every few minutes as I bumped around in the back of the wagon.

The only time mom flinched was when she first saw the blood. Then the serious side of my mother took over. She was concerned, and started barking out orders to everyone. I was surprised she didn't yell at me. When she didn't yell, it made me more scared.

Luckily for me, Dr. Thatcher's medical clinic was very close. The doctors worked for hours to save my ankle and reattach the tendons. To this day I can't feel anything within the whole top of my ankle where that injury happened so many years ago. I have a four-inch-thick scar over the top of my right ankle to remind me of that day. Scars remind us that we were saved from a terrible life threating injury. Some worse than others.

"Do you know how lucky you are?" Dr. Thatcher, the doctor who delivered me, said to me. He repeated it again so I'd get it. "Do you know, Susan Ann, just how lucky you are, and how close you came to losing your foot?"

He whispered to my mother, "She's lost a lot of blood but take her home and she'll build it back up real soon."

My mother nodded in the exam room.

My mom loved Dr. Thatcher, and at that point, he walked on water.

"Everyone else has all the girls," he said to my mother. I remembered hearing her say, "Dr. Thatcher was a proud father to six boys. Those six boys all had boys too," she'd say with fondness. My mom had kept in contact with him over the years and was sad when he passed away about thirty years later. "I loved that man, and what a great doctor he was."

At that age, I really didn't have any clue how lucky I was that day. My foot was still attached to my leg and that fact alone made me happy!

Somehow the knowledge of being lucky to have my foot that day meant a great deal. Today, I can I see how it skewed and reinforced my youthful and reckless thinking of beating death again. I'm not sure if I thought about it deeply in any conscious way, or whether I provoked it with risky behavior. More likely it felt like I was compelled to see how things worked and didn't think about the possibility of losing and limb or death, like any kid with an outgoing personality and adventurous spirit would.

Now I know that Dr. Thatcher saved more than my foot

that day. He saved me from being physically handicapped for the rest of my life. I'll always be grateful to him.

Chapter Five

1974, I'M FOURTEEN

I've never been a religious person although I was always very curious about it. But then, I've never *not* been curious about anything.

I was hungry for knowledge about religion and had no idea what spirituality was as a child, or that there was a difference with the two, religion and spirituality. I understood more about the two than I realized from being in nature. Nature was where I felt more alive than anywhere else, and for sure more alive and connected than while in any church I'd ever been in.

I grew up with no religion and only went to church a handful of times at an Episcopal church on random Sundays every couple of years when my mother felt particularly religious, which was not very often.

As I was celebrating my fourteen birthday, I made friends with a girl across the street from where we lived. Her name was Cathy, and soon after she befriended me, we started going to school together and hanging out afterward. We were becoming great friends.

I was more of a tomboy and Cathy was a girl's girl. She

taught me how to paint my nails, do steamed facials with herbs and all of the girl stuff I'd missed out on. My older sister never did any of that stuff. My 'wardrobe' consisted of boy jeans and sweat jackets in two colors, grey and black.

On one particular day Cathy asked me, "Do you want to learn about Jesus, and be saved?" We were sitting on her blue carpet cross legged Indian style after we'd just painted our nails. I loved learning girly things from Cathy, she had a wealth of information from her mother who sold natural products about staying young and pretty. God, I wanted to be pretty.

It felt like belonging to a special club to me.

"Yeah." I said. Of course, I wanted to learn about Jesus. No one has ever asked me this before. She took out a tiny paper pamphlet with a picture of Jesus on the front and told me the pamphlet was mine once I went through it with her.

"This pamphlet helps us read everything you need to hear, so I'll read it to you and then you say yes when I ask you a question. When we get to the end, that is where you accept Jesus into your life. He loves you," she said airing her nails to get them dry.

I'd heard that before but I didn't know anything about Jesus, or Mary or any of the others in the church. The only thing I knew was a prayer I grew up with at night. It went like this:

Now I lay me down to sleep.
I pray the Lord my soul to keep.
If I should die before I wake,
I pray the Lord my soul to take.

I didn't care for any of the lines especially because I wanted to keep my own soul, and not die before I wake. I told Cathy I stopped that prayer a few years ago. She wasn't interested in trying to analyze my prayer. She wanted to tell me how Jesus was going to save me and I was intrigued, especially about the part where he already loved me.

How could Jesus love me if he didn't even know me? I thought. Cathy mentioned that Jesus loved me so much because he loves all the children and wants to save everyone. It was all foreign to me, and I wasn't sure I needed saving, but the fact that a religious being loved me and wanted to save me was exciting. As Cathy went through the little pamphlet, I noticed her silver painted nails turning the pages required to save me. My nails were red. She was so girly, and I was so not. I wanted to be like her. How did she know all these things I'd never heard of? I'd have to stick close to her and learn as we started looking and liking boys. We both had boy crushes.

She kept asking questions, and I was required to reply yes to each one. I diligently answered Cathy's questions. As she read it to me, it felt so secretive.

"So, how does it feel to be saved?" she asked when she finished reading.

"Okay, I think." Her coconut scent blonde hair fell over my arm when she handed me the pamphlet. Mission completed.

I wanted to give my life to Jesus, so I did, and so I was saved. It was apparently that easy.

I still have the pamphlet to this day because it all felt secret, and special, and a little awkward, but she shared it with me because she cared about me, and that meant the world to me.

As I aged, I took *being saved by Jesus* as seriously as a four-teen-year-old takes anything serious, and still felt a gaping hole in my belief and faith system. There were a lot of rules with the Christian faith and it was expected that I had to go to church with Cathy and her family all the time. Sometimes I enjoyed it but felt embarrassed when I only had one dress that I wore over and over again every Sunday. I didn't continue being a born-again Christian, but I did continue my friendship with Cathy. We are friends to this day.

Many years later I was curious about what I'd learned in some classes I took in high school on all faiths and religions.

I still wanted to know about all of them, and figured it might take me the rest of my life to do so.

Chapter Six

My mother had remarried for the fourth time when I was a junior in high school and I decided to join her for a short visit during Christmas vacation in Wheatridge, Colorado. I'd been living with Cathy's family after my mom moved. Her single mother was kind enough to take me in while I was working and trying to finish high school in Oceanside. I was so grateful. My sister stayed too with another family and my younger brother went with my mom.

I'd never lived in a cold climate and flew over in my platform sandal shoes and light clothing. Once the climate and I met full of beautiful white snow and cold, I bought a jacket as soon as I landed but continued to wear my sandal shoes until I got a cheap pair of sneakers.

A group of teenagers in the area invited me on a rock-climbing adventure. I jumped at the chance to get out with others my age and I wanted to see the rocks of Colorado. I kept my passion for rock collecting since I was little so it seemed like the right afternoon out for me.

After a twenty-minute ride south, we arrived at a place with stepping rocks to climb on, some twenty stories or more high. You were supposed to be able to step to and from each flat rock and reach the top then come back down. I heard there were terrific views at the top.

Though some of us almost made it to the top, most turned back down after ten or so. I was at the head of the group. I almost made it and wanted to push myself so I could see the views but I was starting to get shaky. I hadn't eaten much that day and felt my blood sugar was down.

"I'm stopping here." I said when one of the rocks slipped and fell down some fifteen floors to the rocky ground below. One of the rocks was clearly unsafe so I knew to come back down and not move ahead. I stopped and waited. I'd taken some steps sideways to get out of where I was but I soon became stuck. I had forgotten the path I took up as I turned around to see where I had made it to. One friend was right behind me but did not take the last step I did. When I looked at the step I needed to take to go down, it had no steps in between. It was all air and easy to go up, but not down. We had no rock-climbing equipment and last time I checked I couldn't fly.

Looking down at the ground, I had to be at least 15 floors high, which was about 120 feet. I moved the weight of my body to find a stable place to sit so I wouldn't accidentally fall over.

"Susan, I'm going down," the friend behind me said. "It's getting windy. Let's go home."

"I can't. I can't move," I said intently. "That rock right there is too far away for me to move onto."

"I'm outta here. Sorry," the person said, climbing down. "I need a joint."

"Okay, wait," I said, trying to muster up enough courage to jump from one rock to another downward with nothing, absolutely nothing to hold onto. If I fell, I'd most certainly die or seriously hurt myself. I couldn't move my body. I was frozen with fear. I kept down low trying to stay out of the wind.

I looked out onto the mountains in the distance and nightfall was approaching. I thought about maybe asking the kids to get me a helicopter somehow then realized how silly or impossible that might be.

Everyone was down at the bottom of the rock steps and I was still stuck at the same place. I couldn't reach over to the next rock so I could lower the gravity of my body and slither over to the rock. It was just a foot or so out of reach for me to lower myself onto it. If I was going to get there, I'd have to hop over.

Dammit, I can't do it. Oh my God, I'm going to die, I thought. *I don't even know these people so they'll probably leave me out here alone.*

"Come ooooonnnnnn, Susan," another said.

I took in a deep breath and let it out slowly. It was getting dark fast.

"You guys!" I yelled. "This is really dangerous. I'm literally scared to jump because I might fall." I said almost crying now, but knew crying would not help my situation.

"I'm pretty sure you don't have a choice, Susan," a boy's voice said. "You'll have to jump or hop to the next rock just below you."

So instead of thinking about it too long, and as I studied the rocks, I knew I'd have to take a low leap onto the next rock to get down. If I thought about it any longer, I knew I could talk myself out of it and I'd be there all night long. That'd prove to be very uncomfortable.

I targeted in my mind eye where I needed to land on the rock and kept my body stiff so I could claw the next rock if I slipped. I think my eyes were closed, too, but can't remember for sure. I held my breath and I jumped to the next rock. I hit my knees so hard that I was sure they'd be bruised forever, deep bone bruised.

The part of me that made the choice so quickly was the one I knew I had to follow so I wouldn't be stuck in time making a decision. I climbed down all of the rocks safely but could barely walk once I made it to dirt. I was so relieved and saw that I was so close to falling to my death. It would have happened so fast.

Sure, I knew better and it was a mistake to go up so high. I felt so much relief to be off the mountain of rocks. I had a new appreciation for life, for a while, anyway.

Why? Why did I do such a stupid thing? Because sometimes I do stupid things? It's impossible to know. Because, after all, I was just a teenager. Did I do it because I love the thrill of being alive? Sometimes we have to make those fast choices in life, the ones where your brain doesn't have time to catch up with what you're doing to possibly talk you out of a bad choice, or where you don't have time to think too much about the consequences or what might happen. It's that split second of time in space where time stands still when you make those quick life decisions.

I grew up with a resentment of authority. Non-conformity was my middle name, and I believed that is why I was such a risktaker, I didn't want to follow the rules. I wanted to make my own rules. I aligned it with anything new and exciting of things I was interested in as long as it was and on the cutting edge of technology, count me in.

You'd think these thoughts would keep me locked up at home, but it did just the opposite. I took chances and risks all the time, not thinking they were risks for me.

Everything I did, even as a child, was to extremes. I strived to be better than anyone else and if I put my mind to whatever it might be that I was deciding to do, I would usually come out on top, and if I didn't, I'd work harder, longer, and I never gave up.

But sometimes when someone put me down, deliberately tore down my self-worth, it took years for me to get back up. I'm sure some of this inability to rebound quickly stems from personality and self-esteem, but never being enough was something that was drilled into me constantly when I was young.

Despite my belief in my strength and invincibility, I also had a belief running while I was young and growing up that whatever I did was never enough. No matter what it was. I'd vacuum the carpet but it wasn't good enough.

My stepfather would roar that it wasn't clean enough and I'd find myself on all fours with the small attachments going over every square inch all the way across then down like an old typewriter going back and forth, back and forth.

If I didn't clean the linoleum the right way, and it seems I never did, I'd find myself with a toothbrush to the floor cleaning out every nook and cranny until somehow it was acceptable.

One specific time, I was told to go out into the knee-deep weeds in the back yard that was half the length of a football field and pull all the weeds. I thought the whole thing just needed a big lawnmower.

"You don't just cut the weed you have to pull it up by its roots or it will just grow back faster and fuller. You'll stay here until it is all done, and everything is pulled up by the roots," my stepfather said.

I was definitely the caretaker of the family. I still remember that girl, finding a way to make peace and make everyone happy— no matter what. A girl who had a dream to learn to play the guitar then travel around the world happy and carefree.

My mother had a saying for this about me all throughout my childhood: "Susan can step in pile of shit and come out smelling like a rose."

Whenever I heard my mother say that, I always wondered why I had to step in shit at all. But I believed it. Every word. I believed I could do anything.

I was a master people-pleaser and I grew up striving for an extraordinary life. It may seem admirable to some, but for me, it would later prove to almost end my life for good.

Chapter Seven

I'M IN MY EARLY TWENTIES

Honestly, this time in my life was a blur. I simply can't remember a lot of those dark-night-of-the-soul years. They seemed to all cling together in a big huge dark raincloud, one that might burst at any time.

Occasionally, but not that often, I think about the woman I was in my early twenties. I remember what it felt like to be that age, and for a split-second I saw that part of it felt like a delayed childhood. Everything was new and fun, but I was a mess. I had no idea who I was, and my self-esteem was absent. I didn't know who I wanted to be and it felt like I was just existing day to day.

I was dating Robert, who would become my first husband, and we were both into the 80s world of experimenting with recreational drugs and alcohol. We met at a trendy bar in southern California when I was twenty. The environment of drugs and alcohol were convenient for me because it all helped me numb everything that was trying to surface from my childhood. My eating habits were awful and I usually topped off every dinner with a pint of Häagen-Dazs ice cream, which over time typically became my whole dinner.

What exactly were my days like, the patterns of my

thinking? Sometimes it's hard to recapture this young woman's spirit, impossible to remember how I was feeling, if feeling at all, day after day while forging ahead in the face of possibly being addicted to drugs like cocaine and pot, and with such instability with my sense of self. My life was full of parties, one after the next. We'd drink one after another and started mixing it with anything we could get our hands on.

Somehow, I held down a few random reception jobs or office work, went to college when I liked the class and dropped the ones like logic, that I didn't like. I didn't feel it was logical at all and way too mathematical. I would continue to avoid math in my life at all cost. I often wished I had someone, a mentor, who would step up and call me on my shit and set me straight.

I called my mom under the guise of complaining about something, and then just straight out asked her for rent money for the next month. I'd come up short because my drug habit was becoming a problem. I was fast becoming the girl who ran out of money before payday.

"Mom, I hate to ask you this but… I need some money. Just a little."

"Honey, I don't have it," she said. I knew she wasn't that good with money and usually never had any. I felt bad asking her, but I had no one else to ask.

It was both the first time and the last time I ever asked her for money. She didn't give it to me which is probably the best thing she could have ever done for me. I had to figure it out for myself.

I'd have random reoccurring dreams. One specific one kept happening. I'd be on a ship and I was a pirate. There was always a specific sword fight between me and another pirate. The pirate would take his sword and stab it right through my body. I'd notice what happened, and knowing I was probably dead or should be dead, I'd take that sword and pull it right back out of my body – with no blood being spilt – and say, "Aye, not this time!" And, it was like nothing had ever happened. That specific event was an automatic re-do over and over again.

Back then I remember feeling a tinge of fear about death. The older I got, the more fearful and aware I was about it… death. I never liked gory things, or things that scared me like scary horror movies. My imagination served me well too after those movies, and I could come up with a lot of other things the storyteller never thought or dreamed of. I scared myself with my own imagination.

I'd bring my bed covers up to my nose and I'd dream of being consumed in a house fire. I would act out being in a fire, and what would I do if I was right in the middle of a huge fire. I'd dream about how and when I would die. Most of the time I always lived through it. During some reoccurring dreams I'd fly away from danger, that happened a lot well into adulthood.

Into my twenties, I'd bring up the possibility of horrific accidents like being hit dead-on in a car accident, or getting hit by a fast-moving train while I tempted fate playing on the train tracks. Or I'd slip on some dirt and rocks while I was climbing seemingly unclimbable rocks on the peak of a cliff and fall to my death onto jagged rocks jutting out of a deep blue sea. I was always by myself, and I'd always try to find a way to get out of whatever the impending danger was.

I often wondered if people thought or had dreams like I did.

When I was about twenty-four, I'd gone too far. I was starting to tip over the edge, and was feeling paranoid all the time. I wasn't taking care of myself at all. I had a random paranoia attack at the grocery store feeling like all the things on the shelves were going to fall in on me. I cowered in the corner of one of the aisles to the point that the manager was going to call 911.

"No, don't. I'm fine. I'll leave because I'm not feeling well." They let me leave.

My face and body were starting to change. I was losing weight and didn't look like me any longer due to the drugs I was using. I was about to lose myself for good with drugs. I was losing myself.

I looked into the bathroom mirror in my small apartment and said, "Who are you?"

I had no idea. I remember vividly that lost look in my eyes to this day. I was dressed in a white V-neck cotton T-shirt that definitely wasn't very white. I was breaking out with acne. I hit bottom, and I hated myself.

"Who are you?" I demanded again looking intensely at the mirror. I made a tight and mad fist and slammed it against the mirror.

My reflection looked back at me lost and bewildered, but I saw a little part of that little girl inside of me. She wanted to be saved, and only I could save her.

"That's it, no more!" I said to myself. My words echoed inside the room. "NO MORE!" I realized a few weeks later that I had more than enough love inside of myself to save myself.

That day I swore off recreational drugs for good, and never went back. Years later, I have an occasional alcoholic drink on social occasions.

The steps I took then were small, like learning what I loved most and going out to do them, and I did it even if I was alone. I kept a journal for my recording my feelings. I reconnected with my dreams and what I wanted in life.

I talked with a psychologist who helped me on the journey back to find myself. I learned so much from her: The biggest thing was that being a *people pleaser* was part of healing the inner child. I'm pretty sure I answered every single question of the '25 signs you might have a wounded inner child' with a *yes, that's me.* Trust was a huge issue. I was a rebel and felt more alive when I was in conflict with others. I didn't trust anyone, especially myself.

I had a lot of inner work to do and many long, dark nights of the soul to remember and acknowledge what I've accomplished to the present time in my life. It was a slow process and it would take another thirty years to fully grasp who I was as a woman, as well as to continue to heal my inner child.

"Baby steps," my therapist would say smiling, "Baby steps."

Chapter Eight

I married my first husband, Robert, at twenty-five. Four years later we decided to have a child. At that point in my life, I had a huge desire to get pregnant and be a mother. I did everything I knew to make it happen. I wanted it right away, but fertility doesn't work that way. Robert and I then decided what we needed was a vacation in Hawaii.

It was a great vacation for a childless couple with a lot of drinking, fun, and touristy things to do through three of the islands.

As we started our journey back home, I had a terrible yeast infection. It was not unusual for me to have one because I usually ate too much sugar and yeast thrives on sugar. I was a chocolate chip cookie and chocaholic. While we were checking into our flight at the airport, suddenly, upon the thought of boarding the plane, a fear for my life took over my mind and body. I was scared to death to fly and the fear was so intense I still recall the horrible feeling of dread to this day. My skin registered heat, then cold, and I didn't know how to process this huge fear.

"I have no idea why I'm so scared to fly right now, Robert. I'm terrified." I said with a sweating forehead.

"You've never been afraid to fly," Robert said, surprised, all the while looking at me like *what is wrong with you?* He would keep looking at me again and again to make sure I was getting on the flight with him. I kept trying to be last and so maybe I could make a break for it and run.

I literally had to push myself onto the flight, the fear was that overwhelming. The only reason I pushed was because I knew I needed medical attention for the yeast infection. Back in the day, Monistat was only available in prescription form so there was a hurdle to manage to get treatment.

I went to visit my OBGYN the day I returned from my two-week trip to Hawaii. I was terribly uncomfortable with the yeast infection and the itch was so intense that I could barely contain myself. If I had a rake, I might have used it.

My doctor, a woman from India whom I adored, told me we'd have to run a pregnancy test before she wrote a prescription. I said, "Yes, please do but I should be getting my period soon or maybe I'm a few days late, I can't remember. I'd love to have a baby but I don't think it's positive and I can't feel anything but the itch!"

"Okay, she said. "You never know, till you know." She went off to do the tests and came back into the exam room.

"Susan, you are so pregnant that the test couldn't have bubbled more and it turned bluer than I've ever seen." She looked at me with gloves on, hands up, and her face full of surprise that I couldn't have known I was pregnant.

I was gobsmacked. "Happy" wasn't good enough. "Deliriously happy" was a good start. I was beside myself with joy. I'm pretty sure I even skipped out of her office, talking to the baby all the way home. I talked with my baby that day, and every day for all those months and could not wait to become a mother.

All of the careless thoughts I had about tempting death or reckless behavior stopped when I became pregnant and definitely stopped once my children were born. I was sure it started the moment my body knew I was pregnant; even though I did not know yet, it seems that day at the airport when fear hit hard and I didn't want to get on the plane my body knew somehow. Was I suddenly fearful because I was pregnant? I don't know, I could never explain it any other way but it seemed possible that's what happened.

The force of maternal love was a greater force than perhaps all others. The thought of actually being pregnant was beyond anything I could have hoped for. I was becoming a mother. I was going to be someone's mother. I was now responsible for a tiny little human being inside my body. Someone needed me. I was head over heels in love and couldn't wait for our little one to be born.

Nine months later after a glorious, healthy pregnancy came my first son, Brian. Once he was born my life changed dramatically. *I was a mother.* My life suddenly had meaning and I was responsible for this beautiful bouncing bundle of baby boy, all 8 pounds and 14 ounces of him. I was deeper in love at first sight. We both worked hard during birth and developed fevers. Despite the fever Brian continued to awe his OBGYN with his newborn strength while we were in the nursery.

"Hello, little one," I would say. He doesn't look up from what he's doing but continues to be mad and wail, waiting for attention. Holding my child, I realized my vulnerability to death.

"Oh my God," she said. "Look! he's holding himself up with his arms looking around the nursery."

And he was doing exactly what she said just a few hours after birth. He was up on both arms and you could see his cute little fingers with those adorable newborn dents on them looking around for his momma, or perhaps more likely, some food. His hair was swept up in a little swirl on the top of his head.

He also had the thighs of a six-month-old and the appetite of four babies right when he came out of my body. I could barely keep him fed. My breastmilk wasn't enough. He'd cry for more food all of the time.

It felt like I was the only mother to ever live, and I loved being a mother. Logically, of course, I knew I wasn't the only woman to ever have a child, but something happened to me when I became a mother. There wasn't anything I couldn't do after giving birth. It gave me life. I adapted the 'mama bear' mentality almost immediately.

Once I became a mother, it felt like there was a part of myself outside of my body. I realized there is a unique and beautiful connection, like an invisible umbilical cord of emotion between mother and child that is always there from the moment they are born. I felt it intensely, it built up during pregnancy, and it became manifest instantly once he was born. It's a lot like a quote I've heard many times and memorized:

"Making the decision to have a child is momentous. It is to decide forever to have your heart go walking around outside your body."
-Elizabeth Stone

Upon giving birth and holding my new bundle of joy while I was recovering, my thoughts went out to women who were not as fortunate as I was. Women who could not get pregnant or carry a child and become a mother. I felt a sense of sadness for these women. They could adopt or choose to have a child many different ways in the world today, of course, and it was up to them as to how they'd want to build their family. I felt strongly they should have as many choices as possible. Maybe they wanted and desired that biological connection and couldn't carry their own child. I felt a strong desire to help them.

Women gave birth every day, but did they feel like I did? Did their lives change so dramatically like mine did?

A month or so after my son's birth, and after the immersion deep into motherhood, feeling the good and the bad, the ups and the downs, the struggles of having a child, and remembering my childhood, I called my mother who lived in northern California. I was crying and so overwhelmed at what being a mother really meant.

"I'm so sorry for all the things I've ever done to you, Mom. I love you."

My mother said, "This is a welcomed, although years later wake-up call for you Susan. You'll be a wonderful mother. I Love you too."

Chapter Nine

The second time I gave birth, I experienced the same feeling of overwhelming motherly love with the invisible emotional connection attached to and within me to my new baby. That connection remains steadfastly strong as the baby needs you, and later wanes as you let go as your children become adults, but the bond is always there for they are always your babies, your children, no matter how old they are.

I was elated to have a second son, Steven.

My boys were everything to me. I was a mother again! Steven was strong, too, and in perfect health. One day after we were back at home from the hospital, he showed me how strong he was. I was a little late with his bottle and he got furious. My boys were demanding when it came to food. Breastfeeding wasn't enough for him either so I supplemented with formula. I placed him on a little blanket while I prepared his bottle and he was so mad he wasn't getting food right away, he cried so hard his little eight-pound newborn body tensed up so much that his strength turned his whole body completely over at fifteen days old! I was amazed!

Now I was a mother to two sons. I felt so happy, so alive, and so motherly. I often thought about women who could not have children given I was so lucky to effortlessly get pregnant and have children.

As the boys grew into toddlers, I became aware of myself more as a mother. It was difficult to find myself as a woman because the lines of identity between being a woman and a mother blended so well together. My self-identity could be easily lost when I absorbed myself into mothering. I never knew I was lost until I was confused, and so I went looking for myself. To make it more complex, being a wife was another identity.

When I couldn't make that differentiation, my life changed dramatically because fear would take over when I couldn't see who I was, my own self-identity. It seemed to be more present with two toddlers. Clearly, motherhood was different than being single and only worrying about yourself. I would protect my children with my life.

All of my life, I seemed be afraid of the other shoe falling. When things were so wonderful, I waited and wondered what would happen now because I was so happy.

So, I would foresee dangerous situations like when a car is backing up in a parking lot and the driver is not paying any attention to anything around them. I'd quickly point it out to others, or put my arm in front of them to stop them from getting hurt and keep them safe. I still do that to this day, especially with my children. I see potential accidents before they happen, probably because I thought about it too much as a child, or I had a keen intuitive insight that I never quite believed I had. I'd see situations where things 'might' happen. Some did happen and some did not. I had a very overactive imagination along with my strong intuition.

As a mother it worked well for keeping my kids safe, but it never worked for me to see the danger in almost everything, it made me too careful.

Sometimes I was so highly aware of the potential of danger that it seemed I carried it around with me everywhere.

I was more fearful for others than I was for myself, even though I often thought and dreamed about what it would be like when I die. What would happen? And how would it happen? What would happen afterward?

Chapter Ten

1993, I'M THIRTY-THREE

I put my religious beliefs on the back burner until I met my first husband, Robert. He was Catholic, and I'd never set foot in a Catholic church except by accident one time when my mother drank too much vodka straight from the bottle at the San Luis Rey Mission, and I found myself sitting in the pews with the fathers until my mother sobered up enough to drive us home. She went there looking for refuge, a shoulder to cry on, and to help herself. She eventually found it and sobered up through AA, Alcoholics Anonymous when I was thirteen.

There was one catch to marrying my first husband, Robert.

"My mom and dad, along with my family and the church would require you to become Catholic." Robert said one night while we lay in bed.

I would have to officially join his faith so we could be married in the Catholic Church. I was okay with it because I thought it'd be good to learn about Catholicism, and then Robert and I would have more in common. *Maybe we'd get closer as a couple?* I thought. I went to classes and went through the pre-marriage requirements, things seemed fine and I 'graduated' to marry in the church. It was good for a while anyway.

As I grew within myself in many ways, I started to see this

new faith as a barrier that had lots of rules and regulations. There was now a list of things one could not do, things that would be considered a sin. There were now these rules to follow including rules about attending mass every single Sunday. I had always wondered why you had to attend church if you believe your faith within your heart.

As Robert and I had children, he wanted them to go to Catholic school and I did not. I was an independent thinker and didn't mix well with institutional religion telling me how I should and shouldn't be, what I should and shouldn't think or believe.

There was particular incident that turned me hard away from being Catholic. We were in church one Sunday, all four of us on a beautiful summer day. We usually sat up in the cry room because at the time our second son was still a baby. That day we ventured out into the church because our littlest, Steven was sleeping in my arms.

The priest, Father John, was talking about abortion. He said, "There was a woman who came in to see me, and didn't know what to do about the baby in her belly. Presumably she'd been raped by her father."

I was horrified at first because of his use of the word "presumably." Did he know for sure, or was he questioning the account? How could any of us know what happened to her or what the truth of the matter was?

The church went silent as that got the whole congregation's attention, and you could hear a pin drop. He was very adamant and unwavering in his conviction up in the pulpit. His deep voice was strong and convincing, his arms were moving up and down, at times hitting the pulpit and making loud noises with the microphone as he spoke with authority and what felt like to me like judge and jury.

Father John continued, "She asked me what she should do? I told her she'd be committing a mortal sin if she had an abortion. It is wrong, and she won't be forgiven. She must have the baby."

I was mortified. I wasn't sure I heard what I heard; did he really just say that? I looked at Robert, Robert looked at me. I looked over at other people and they weren't moved. Not like I was. We didn't say anything to each other and then looked at our children.

The instant I heard his words and digested them seconds later, after trying to know if I heard them correctly, then knowing what he actually said, I stood up from the middle pews and moved to the center aisle of the church. I put my hand out and Brian put his hand in mine as I held his brother. I said, "Let's go." I shuffled past everyone giving me the looks of confusion and disbelief.

I thought Robert would follow, but he stayed in the pew as we walked out of the church. I got to the back of the church and glanced over at his head in the crowd. Honestly, I was shocked he decided to stay, but understood he definitely gets to have his own opinion. Whenever we talked about those things, he'd just let me talk and not engage with me on any kind of conversation about it. I felt very strongly about women's choices and right to choose.

Later that day I said to Robert, "A woman should not be shamed into having a child if she doesn't want one, especially if the father is her father!" I was almost begging for him to understand me when he got home from church. Abortion wasn't talked about in my classes to become catholic, and apparently as I found out later, they left a lot of controversial items out of the class.

"There is always adoption," Robert replied. I closed my eyes in response because I knew he didn't understand the situation from the woman's point of view at all.

"Yeah, but she is ruined forever just by what happened to her to result in the pregnancy, Robert, let alone going through pregnancy and birth, and then letting go of the child." I cried. He stood looking at me, not seeing me at all.

"You don't get it, do you? It's her body." I looked at his face for any signs. "And I don't get that you don't get that," I said.

I never set foot in the Catholic Church again. Eventually, Robert and I would divorce. It wasn't an easy divorce, but I guess most aren't. I pulled the boys out of their Catholic school when they were in first grade and kindergarten, and put them into a great public school instead.

Later I was told by many people that many in the Catholic Church do not all think that way, and it was but one opinion, of one priest, who was eighty-six years old and that I "*shouldn't take it so seriously.*" Though there was probably a lot more to the story that I didn't know, I did take it personally because he was talking to a church full of people and it was abhorrent enough to close me off to considering practicing any religion from then on. Even though I don't believe in religions in general, I have a lot of family and friends who are religious and I accept them wholly for who they are, and what they believe.

I still didn't know what the true answer was for me, but I did want some kind of spiritual path to follow. As I learned more about spirituality, I stayed open to the idea of spiritual growth, but not religion.

I started to get very curious about soul connection. I bought all of Gary Zukav's books starting with *The Seat of the Soul.* I was hooked. I wanted answers. What I didn't realize was the answers were already inside of me, and all I had to do was explore within.

I had a hunger to evolve but it would take more dark nights than I ever knew I was able to withstand before that would occur.

Chapter Eleven

1998, I'M THIRTY-EIGHT

This was the year I would end my marriage. It remains one of the hardest things I've ever done in my life.

I fell out of love with the man I promised to love forever. We grew apart and nothing could put us back together again. I tried everything from couple's retreats to counseling. It seemed we crossed the point-of-no-return when he decided to not go to marital counseling any longer. "Maybe you need it more than I do," my husband, Robert said in a hurtful sort of way.

When I said nothing back it was because I'd run out of any answers, and so I thought maybe I did need it more than him. He added, "We don't need counseling or therapy, we can do this ourselves."

I realized how he was partially right, that maybe I did need counseling more than he did.

It was me who changed. Not him.

It was a defining moment for us, and I knew it was the end. He wouldn't or couldn't go forward to help us. I knew I'd have to go it alone.

Suddenly, from all points after what Robert had said, it felt like I was divorced although it took three more years to finalize.

I had no idea how to fall back in love, and questioned if it was it even possible? Could one fall back in love with no tools, no guidance? Can feelings change like that? I simply didn't think so because had I tried.

There were no books on it that I related to or could find that would really give me the answers I sought.

"Once the love is gone from a relationship, it's just gone for good. There is nothing to go back to." A few good friends would tell me when I tried to talk with them about this subject.

Initially I wasn't sure and questioned everything I could think of for the possibility that we might be able to save our marriage.

One thing is for sure, it took *two* to fix a relationship. I couldn't make it work by myself. For some reason I had believed I could fix anything in life, even people. I saw it was definitely a no-win situation. I'd lost what it took to keep my relationship together and started to see that I'd have to divorce my husband, break up our family of four, and leave my relationship and go out into the world as a single mother of two.

As our relationship grew father apart. I fell completely out of love, it felt inevitable. It happened. We tried to make it work, or what I thought of as 'trying,' for three very long years before our divorce was finalized.

I'd have to do this to help myself, my life, because the only thing more unthinkable than divorcing my husband, to me, was the unbearable thought of staying in the marriage. In my view, staying together for our children's sake was a lame reason to stay in a loveless marriage.

I could see myself years in my future thinking I should have done it, I should have left, *I should have. Should have.*

I still had life inside for future love and in that life, I had a strong desire for an intimate soulful love with another person. Yet, I had no idea how to get it.

It remains one of the hardest things I've done in my life, to stare truth down in the middle of my turmoil, bring it all up and into reality and finally find the courage to leave my marriage.

It was time for me to move on, but I had no idea what was in store for us and I knew little about what *moving on* alone really meant with two young children.

I'd end up leaving the family home that we owned together, then lost, due to financial concerns of not being able to talk or communicate with Robert. I lost my job due to Steven having health issues with serious reflux requiring surgery, and Robert gave up paying anything. We were in financial ruin.

The boys and I moved thirteen miles up the coast to a small south bay beach town to start over. It had excellent schools and we would move into a cute little blue-trimmed rental house. Brian was almost eight and Steven had just turned six.

After a very difficult move, we ended up in a children's therapist office the first week of the move because I thought I would burst with guilt and remorse. We only went once but I was glad I made the appointment.

I felt an unbelievable sense of heavy guilt for tearing apart our family. I worried about how my choice would affect my boys. I felt I had to give them every tool possible to deal with the divorce and help them navigate it. I didn't want to be a "broken family," and would learn years later we were never broken at all, just rearranged and changed.

The children's therapist read a children's book to the boys to break the ice and I believe it did. The book was called, *A Family Divorce*. I don't remember a lot of the book but I do remember crying my eyes out in the background while they were gazing at the pages, the boys would look over at me then look at the book again. They watched me shed many tears that day.

It felt like I let them down, that I didn't give them the family scene they so deserved. It gave me a freedom I couldn't describe, and I wanted so desperately and needed as a woman. It's a bittersweet memory that will stay with me for all of my days.

We stopped by the beach on the way home. The sea was flat under a grey overcast sky. The waves pounded the sand and sprayed up white foam each time they hit. The boys ran free on the sand barefoot throwing a football to each other. While I spread a blanket to sit down, the sudden feeling that I made the right choice washed over and though my whole body.

I looked down and saw a white feather on the sand, wondering where it might have come from. The wind swept it up onto the top of my hand while I rested on the blanket. I stared at it and thought about what the meaning of a white feather might be. I remembered it meant many different things like angels are near or new beginnings. All were good symbols to me.

After about twenty minutes, the boys made their way over to where I was sitting. They were sweating and tired from running around the beach as they hit the blanket to sit with me.

Steven looked at the top of my hand at the small lone white feather.

"Oh mommy, a fevver," he said, pointing to the top of my hand. I looked at him looking at the feather. I stared at my youngest son. I simply couldn't look away. The two missing front baby teeth with new ones growing in, and the last part of the little boy I'll see as he grows up so fast. I look over at his brother, already growing up into a fine young man, and at that very moment I'm so proud as their mother.

"Yes, a feather," I softly say, as I reflected upon the moment.

I took the feather and lifted it high above my head, and both boys looked up to watch. I waited for a strong breeze to take it away. As I let go, all three of us watched it fly far away, the wind took it up, up and away. It flew into the sky.

"It's gone." Steven said.

"Yes honey, it's gone, and everything is going to be okay."

Chapter Twelve

A decade later, after I was *done* having eight babies for five other families with surrogacy, I had this wild idea that I wanted to be the best me I could be. I declared it was time for me.

While I was a surrogate mother for ten years, I never once feared for my life while I was pregnant. Being pregnant for me was like snuggling up on the couch with your favorite blanket, a good book, and some hot chocolate or coffee. Every single pregnancy always went well, and there were never any medical problems. I was unbelievably grateful my body could withstand pregnancy the way it did.

When people were concerned for me at work, or others would mention to me about doing *so many surrogacies*, I'd feel good about it, not bad. I felt like I was a strong woman, not one who couldn't manage her life and her body. I knew the dangers, and was sure the downside or health issues would not happen to me.

I found my unique abilities in being a mother and a surrogate mother. I was somewhat obsessed, or even addicted to surrogacy and did it over and over again, not realizing I might have been tempting fate every single time I got pregnant.

Secretly, I also loved the fact that growing and birthing a

child and assisting God in a miracle and the one thing a man could not do.

I admit that being a surrogate mother gained me attention, though admittedly not always the good kind, but attention nonetheless. I got a very intimate sense of self-satisfaction with what I did and always did it with a win-win intention.

I could be and I was finally ready and open to having a relationship with another person. I wanted to focus on my life and me for once.

The boys were getting older, and after I'd done a lot of work on my inside which included my self-esteem issues for years, I was fairly lucky that the outside bounced back pretty well after seven pregnancies.

It was an ongoing thing to work on both the inside and the outside at the same time. My C-section left a scar with a little flap of skin. It bothered me a lot and did not want to just get used to it. It wasn't your normal healing from a C-section. There was additional scar tissue under the skin, pushing it out into a flap like an envelope flap and it was driving me crazy.

The scar wasn't flat at all, or in a straight line like a lot of women's C-section scars are. Some women were fortunate enough that you couldn't even see their scars at all after a number of years. Not mine. It was there every time I took my clothes off, every time I had a shower, bothering me every time. I became really self-conscious and could not get plastic surgery off my mind. I wanted a surgeon to fix that flap, to take it off, and flatten the scar. Apparently, I didn't work enough on myself inside to be happy with myself outside. I wasn't totally comfortable with my body, and thought, *I'd just be happy if I fixed that C-section.*

Research was essential to see what could be done, and I'd already read a lot of self-help books. Apparently, I didn't read the one to accept yourself exactly as you are, body and all. I must have ignored those books because I still wanted to change my body, not accept it just as it was.

This is hard to write about because I never thought of myself as vain, or I just didn't want to see it in myself. Now, accepting that, despite that, I just wanted to feel better about my body, so I decided to do it.

I met with two plastic surgeons in the area where I lived. I was hoping to be excited or thrilled after the consults and about them as doctors, but that wasn't the outcome: They didn't want to just take the skin off.

"You can't just go in and fix that, you need to have a whole tummy tuck." they both said. I didn't think I needed something that extensive. I kept searching.

I talked with my OBGYN at my last postpartum visit.

"Only a plastic surgeon can do that type of surgery." It felt like I wasn't going to get what I wanted unless I went to a plastic surgeon.

I kept all this to myself because I was afraid people would think I was a self-absorbing freak. But I thought to myself, they didn't have this problem, I did. I joined a couple groups on Facebook and talked with other women that had concerns about their C-section scars too. There were very few that shared my same problem.

I'd had some therapy in the past so I began applying what I had learned by constantly asking myself, "Why do I need to do this?" I felt I needed to justify it to myself. The answer that kept coming back to me was, because I want it to feel and look better for myself. That was good enough for me.

I continued to look for a plastic surgeon. At the time "mommy makeovers" were a thing. But I just wanted one thing, I didn't want three or four different things and most definitely didn't want the high surgical cost of a full mommy makeover.

I ended up at a Beverly Hills facility to see Dr. Raden. Apparently, he was the plastic surgeon to the stars in Hollywood. I thought he must be good if the celebrities were going to him to get work done. It worked to impress me but at the end of the day, I only wanted the best surgeon and the best laid out plan for the lowest cost.

Dr. Raden's office was basic black and white, a clean masculine look with a lot of celebrity photos of himself and them. He had grown his practice for almost twenty years. I wasn't so struck by this celebrity status, and found I really liked him as a person. He gave off a good, warm vibe. During our appointment he seemed thoughtful, easy-going, professional, and gave me the information I needed to move forward. He also had started a non-profit and helped troubled youth and gangs get rid of unfortunate tattoo choices with his surgical expertise. He had all the qualifications and more.

"I can do a partial tummy tuck for you to hide the flap. But we can't just cut it off because of how it will need to be folded into your body," he said, flashing his Hollywood smile that somehow still had a hint of humility to it. It was endearing, until he suggested that maybe I could use a new set of breasts, too.

I was sitting on the exam table, and he was standing. He moved to get something from a cabinet and came over to me. "You'd look great with these," he said, putting a silicone implant up under my breast, moving and adjusting it just so.

My breast looked quite different with a handsome man giving it an instant, younger look. But I wasn't sold. I was rather fond of my breasts and did not need new ones, though I dare say it was an inviting thought.

"No, I don't think I need those," I said to Dr. Raden turning down the upsell from the good doctor. I wanted one thing and made the appointment to have the surgery.

A month later, I had the procedure at an outpatient facility.

After the surgery, I recalled Dr. Raden talking to me during the procedure while I was under anesthesia, but I barely remembered what he said. It was all foggy, my mind wasn't really awake and sleep was the only thing I wanted. He asked me a question, something about having babies in the future.

Something like "are you planning on any more pregnancies?"

"What?" I had responded, groggy. It was a question along the lines of having *more children*. Of course, the answer from me was a resounding "no." at that time because I was single and thought it wouldn't happen for me again. That ship had sailed, the boys were grown, and surrogacy was in my past. It was all a bit fuzzy and I couldn't remember exactly what he asked. I didn't give it another thought because it didn't apply to my current life.

I was somewhat happy with the outcome of the surgery but it still didn't look the way I hoped it would. I got used to my new reality and made peace with my body. I was happy I didn't have the puff of tissue just below my navel and knew it would a while before I would see the long- term results.

Chapter Thirteen

2010, I'M FORTY- NINE

Twelve years later, after the end of a painful divorce, I found love again. But this time it was different. I was ready and open to a new relationship. My boys were now older and more self-sufficient, and it was finally time for this single mother. I'd learned how to live with myself, really got to know myself, and most importantly love myself.

I finally got serious about dating and put myself back out there again after all my surrogate journeys.

But let me tell you it wasn't easy. I'd been yearning and looking for love for a long time and now realized I would never settle until I found the right person, until I was the right person.

Paul and I met on e-harmony in late 2009. He confessed later that I was his 'last try' on an internet dating site. I too confessed to him that he was also my last try. We were fed up with the whole internet dating thing and it hadn't gone anywhere for either one of us.

I often wondered if fate was calling to both of us, that maybe we were supposed to meet at that moment in time. The timing with everything was right for both of us.

We first made contact via computer in August, 2009. Then

we both called off at least three potential dates for one reason or another until we finally met in December that year. Our profiles were sitting in each other's inbox for months. Paul's front profile picture showed him in a snow suit standing next to a helicopter, getting ready to ski down a mountain. I'd thought that was the kind of guy for me, an adventurous, active one. My profile picture was a cropped version of me holding my last set of twins. I did finally add a good picture by the time we got around to having a date. Back in those days, we didn't have camera phones readily available all the time like now.

Just from our profile pictures it was amazing we ever met: I put him off because I had a preconceived judgement that maybe he was a rich guy who could get any girl, and he put me off because I lived in Manhattan Beach, California and thought I was way too high maintenance for him.

We met in the parking lot in front of a little Japanese restaurant. He walked over to introduce himself, we said our hellos, shook hands, and headed toward the restaurant located in a strip mall in Redondo Beach, California.

From the moment I met Paul, everything felt so comfortable. First, we were both tall, with him a few inches more than my 5-foot, 10-inch frame. (Since this wasn't usually the norm, it seemed, it was a relief he was a little bit taller.) I immediately felt I could completely be myself. We talked for hours on that first date. It felt like I'd known him for years.

The just time flew by in those hours together. We had so much in common, and we talked for nearly four hours in the corner of the little restaurant where a medium sized square fan held the door open for air. We were so balanced in talking about our own lives and taking interest in the other's life with questions and curiosity. When we finally left, he walked me to my car. We didn't kiss, though I really did want to kiss him. I always felt funny about being forward with men, and I wanted this date to go right. I wanted us to work, and knew that I felt ready for a truly healthy relationship.

A week later, Paul asked me out for a second date. We went to P.F. Changs and things became a bit more complicated when he asked more questions right up front about my past. I could tell he must have been thinking about it for some time between our first and second dates.

These things always came up at some point in time on dates. In past dates, whenever I came to the part about being a surrogate mother, most men would start looking for the front door in whatever restaurant we happened to be in thinking about a way out once I told them about being a surrogate mother.

It ended up being the best second date I'd had in ten years. But at first, Paul looked serious and he had questions.

"So, what's wrong... like, why?" he said, struggling to get the words out. He tried to backtrack on his sentence because he'd realized how he said it. "I mean, why were you single for so long?" he asked.

I could see he was genuinely interested. His voice was deep and manly, and full of curiosity.

I knew what he meant because I'd had enough dates to get the gist of it all. He was referring to the fact that I was approaching fifty and still single. He wanted to know why I was *still available*. It was a valid question and probably one I would have asked as well. So, I knew it was coming: The conversation about surrogacy, my surrogate mother past.

This time, however, I felt it would be different than with previous men because this time I was done being a surrogate mother. I wouldn't have to tell him I might be pregnant in the future with someone else's baby while we were together. Because his interest in why I was single for so long was so sincere, I decided to tell him what I'd done for the past decade, the whole decade of my forties.

"Men don't usually want to date a woman who is pregnant all the time," I said. He looked really puzzled.

"This might take a little while, but if you're willing to listen, I'm happy to tell you my story and what I've been up to for ten years."

"Yes, of course. Please do," he said as he pulled his blonde-reddish bangs to the side of his head. He had a moustache to match his hair. His eyes were a gentle blue, caring, and felt loving.

I took a long, deep breath, and began.

After I gave birth to my sons, Brian and Steven, their father and I divorced a few years thereafter. Being a single mother was no easy task, and the thought of a new relationship became chilling because my mother had been married five times. I didn't want to follow in those footsteps. I stepped back with pursuing relationships during that time.

But... I loved being pregnant. I loved it so much that I decided to become a surrogate mother and I gave birth to eight babies, three sets of twins and two singletons, for five different families. His eyes widened after I said this. It was a typical reaction.

I learned that surrogacy was not something to be taken lightly and took a lot of energy; having a child for another couple brought me into unchartered territory, straight into the personal lives of the intended parents. I learned that the match in a surrogacy between intended parents and surrogate was the most important part of the journey.

As I kept doing surrogacy journeys, I wondered when I would know that I was done having children. I began asking my sister, my friends, and anyone who would listen "When will I know?" They'd say, "don't worry Susan, you'll know." I kept waiting, hoping one day I would.

My first two surrogate journeys were for the same couple. After I'd birthed a son for them in 2000, they asked me to be their surrogate again. During our second journey, life became extremely complicated, presenting more problems than I ever imagined. Three embryos were put into me, and all three 'took' making me pregnant with triplets. The parents and two doctors demanded a reduction back down to twins. I didn't want to, and only very reluctantly agreed. My intuition was right: It ended up being a horror story all by itself.

As the due date got closer, the intended parents determined they would divorce and breached out contract. Worse yet, they no longer wanted the twins I was carrying, they never showed up at the hospital after the birth of their healthy boy/girl twins, and left endless financial issues in the aftermath.

I took the twins home with me to fight for parentage and let the courts decide who was their mother instead of surrendering them to Department of Child and Family Services, DCFS. I was the mother… I wasn't the mother… the phrases constantly played in my head during all this. I was *the unexpected mother*. And, I wasn't aware this type of thing could even happen, to me or anyone else, especially when a couple went to such great lengths to have a child. How could they then change their minds?

It's a much longer story, actually, and one that gained some attention from the media. I did a PBS special, People Magazine, and some other outlets, and then Oprah's people found it and my story was told in her magazine in 2003 and became one of her top ten stories in O, The Oprah Magazine in 2010, but that's a whole other story.

(I found out later that Paul would check out my story on the internet and was amazed that what I was saying was in fact, true.)

In spite of this whole hardship with the journey, I still wanted a good experience with surrogacy and after talking to many of my surrogate friends I felt driven to continue, so I decided to try again.

By this time, my boys were used to seeing their mother pregnant and didn't know anything different. I explained everything to them early on.

Tick Toc, Tick Tock, Tick Tock... went the clock. I was forty-one.

My third journey was for a couple who found me through an article about that second journey. They had undergone fifteen failed in vitro fertilizations (IVF) at Cornell and Stanford, the best of the best, only to be disappointed every single time.

I learned the match between a surrogate and the intended parents is the most important part of a surrogate journey. Intuition can be a fabulous human instrument when you listen to it. I connected beautifully with them compared to the first couple, and they became very close to me and my boys. I desperately wanted to help them have a family.

After five IVF failures with me as their surrogate, a renowned infertility specialist said, "Well, maybe it's you, Susan."

After the shock wore off because I actually did think it was me for a while, I became embedded in their infertility issues and really wanted to find out why they could not conceive. I felt challenged and became a Google queen, researching tons of medical documents online, and asked multitudes of questions of the doctor and embryologist. I was relentless. Why can't we get pregnant? What hasn't been done yet?

There had to be an answer. After eighteen months of trying to make a baby, I compiled a checklist. A blood karyotyping test had never been done, something usually done by a geneticist, not an infertility doctor. I begged the doctor to run the test for my intended parents until he finally agreed.

"I'm only doing this to humor you, Susan," our reproductive endocrinologist doctor said, standing in his multi-million dollar decked-out office with all the newest, shiniest furniture and equipment.

The genetic problem was found with the blood test. Upon meeting with the doctor again I'm pretty sure he was humbled down to at least my level for a few hours. We were all happy the genetic problem was found and it was a sperm issue with the intended father, not the mother and why it's so important to do genetic testing *before* you start IVF.

They fixed the medical issue as much as they could with the choices they had at the time and once they had a healthy sperm and egg = embryo, and I became pregnant with twins on our next transfer.

Nine months later, I gave birth to boy/girl twins. I'll never forget the moment I put the twins into their parents' loving arms, one at a time. Their faces reflected the closest to pure joy I've ever witnessed. It was magical for me. I loved what I did, helping to make families. I should have been satisfied.

Tick Tock, Tick Tock... went the clock. I was forty-four.

My fourth journey was for friends of friends. They tried numerous times to conceive. I did my first independent journey (without an agency) because by this time I knew the process.

A pregnancy is very difficult to hide and everyone becomes an expert when they see a woman pregnant. "Oh, is this your first baby?" strangers would ask, rubbing my big, round belly in an elevator. "Oh no, it's my eighth," I'd say. When people at work, I worked in HR Human Resources for a think tank tied to the DOD Department of Defense and NASA. So, when they started asking more questions, I'd explain to human resources and rocket scientists alike all about the surrogacy process.

I knew my time for carrying babies was coming to an end. Each one was healthy, born without complications, and I felt blessed.

I started to wonder about the why of my pregnancies. Why did I need this? What exactly did it give me? If I stayed pregnant, I wouldn't have to try to have a relationship. I dated in between pregnancies, but no man understood my obsession. Additionally, I felt absolutely fabulous being pregnant, better than when I wasn't even. A doctor once told me, "You might be addicted to the hormones, not primarily the pregnancy."

I gave birth to a healthy little boy for my intended parents. It was the fourth time I placed a baby into another woman's arms. It was my choice, my body, and one of the most feminist things I've ever done. To me, nothing was more powerful and meaningful than creating a family.

Tick Tock, Tick… My clock was slowing down, but I still didn't know if I was done having children. Who was supposed to tell me? I was now forty-six.

I returned to my OB/GYN for approval for another surrogacy. He said, "Okay, Susan, one more. That's it! God, I wish all my patients had text book pregnancies like yours."

I thought long and hard, wondering if I should move ahead. I would have to go through all of the shots for twelve weeks, a twenty-two-gauge needle for sticking in the top muscle and fat of my buttocks, the tablets, suppositories, tests, appointments, all of it.

Fat pants, skinny pants, in-between pants. One more time, just one, then I'll start seriously dating, I thought. I remembered the glow I felt when the hormones surged through my veins, and I longed to feel life move inside of me one more time.

"How can you give up a baby you carry?" People often asked me, and maybe that's what you're thinking now. It's difficult to answer unless you feel compelled to be a surrogate mother. You either know you can do it, or you know you can't; there is no in between. The children I bore came through me, but they weren't biologically mine. The bond and connections I've had with my surrogate babies has always been one of love. I realized even my own children are not *mine*. They came through me to be of this world independently, but I was there to guide them, love them, and care for them as their mother.

My fifth journey was for friends of friends, only this time they weren't your typical male and female couple. They were a gay couple, together for fourteen years, who wanted a family. They used an egg donor, splitting the eggs and fertilizing half with each man's sperm. This particular journey opened me up in ways that were unimaginable. I learned that if two men or two women are in love and want to be parents it is purely okay. They are just like heterosexual couples, just with a difference of their sexual orientation.

I really enjoyed this journey very much. We became pregnant with twins on the first try, a biological child from each man and one egg donor, and we gave birth to a sweet little boy and a girl in April 2008.

Tick Tock... went the maturing clock. I was forty-eight.

It was time to hang up my surrogacy shoes. After birthing ten babies, it was time to stop, but I still had the yearning.

I have kept in contact with all of my surrogate babies, except the very first one, the one that went wrong for obvious reasons.

After I told Paul my long-winded story that night on our second date, he looked at me with a serious face. I couldn't tell if he believed me or not. I took a long breath in and let it out slowly. I'd had some pretty awful dates during those ten years, and I hoped my intuition proved right, that maybe we might have another date.

I looked over at him waiting for a reply. The silence was comfortable, felt right. I waited.

I could see tears welling in his eyes. "That's the most beautiful story I've ever heard," he said.

"What a wonderful thing to do for someone else," he said as he swallowed hard. "I've never had children so I wouldn't know what it all entails but wow, what a story."

I moved back from the table in surprise, forgetting all about my meal. I reached for my water and gulped it down, then breathed deeply, feeling a little vulnerable and not knowing what to say next.

He gets it, I thought. To me, he was the first man to understand the beauty of surrogacy and still accept me for who I am. With past dates, and I must have gone through at least twenty-five or more, I had shared this same story and all of them were in disbelief or disapproving of what I was doing with surrogacy. They'd nod and then find a way out of the restaurant and never call me again.

This was my first encounter from a potential mate that understood what I was doing or at the very least accepted me for *me*. We were a lot alike in many ways and very like-minded. He had an incredible sense of humor, he made me laugh.

We sat there staring at each other in such a beautiful moment. I then felt incredibly shy.

He reached across the table and opened his hand for mine. I lifted my hand over the table and silver wear, through the napkins and untouched food to put my hand in his. His hand felt warm, *probably just like his heart*, I thought.

For the next few months, and on every single date with Paul I was getting more and more smitten. For the first time in my life I didn't just jump into bed with a date. I hoped we both would be ready for that when we were ready for that next step, so I spent time examining my former ways, and I consciously changed my narrative to make that happen.

I fell in love with Paul on a bright spring day in March. I remember it so clearly because getting to know one another was opening us up to so much more. We explored many different and new places and we both shared a love of the outdoors. We hiked together, going up mountains in Malibu that left me breathless and sweating. A lot. Maybe for the first time, I didn't care how I looked because Paul and I were enjoying each other, each moment so much. I wondered if he might be the one. The one I could finally have a truly intimate relationship with, someone I could share anything with, and him with me.

Eight months later at fifty years old, in August of 2011, we, along with our guests were barefoot on the beach and Paul and I married in Hermosa Beach, California. We had a beautiful three-tiered cake with starfish and shells on the top from my collection with fifty of our closest friends and family.

Steven had just finished his senior year in high school, getting ready to head to The University of Arizona, and Brian was already in college at Long Beach State University.

Aside from what my friends and family might tell you now, they would have never bet on me getting married so fast.

"Susan, wow, it seems so quick to get married so fast?" I'd often hear at work or through the more distant grapevine. Not one person in my family or my circle of close friends said anything about the timing because they knew me and trusted my decisions, even if I had decided get married within eight months of meeting Paul.

Honestly, I wondered myself if our love happened *too fast*, but I always came back to *you just know, when you know.*

If it feels right and warm in your heart to move forward and love, then it's time to move forward.

Chapter Fourteen

After Paul and I married, we started talking about the possibility of having a child together. It wasn't something I thought I would do. I thought I was done with this part of my life. I was still able to bear a child, but did I want this at this time in my life? It did feel so natural to me though, something I would love to do. But could we, would we? It sounded like a lovely idea, but could it be possible? Would I still be fertile?

Paul had not had a biological child at that point in his life but was fascinated at the possibility. He married 22 years before. His wife suffered a heart attack a few years ago leaving him widowed. She was 15 years older than he, and had two grown step children with their own lives, from her first marriage. Our first conversation went like this:

"Have you ever thought about having children?" I asked Paul.

"Yes, I have many times but I never thought it would happen. I thought it was just something that I wouldn't experience this time around." He said.

After we talked about it a lot, and upon thinking about how it would change our lives, which was now full of freedom and only ourselves, we thought seriously about the possibility of having a child. I was healthy, not on any medications and I felt as healthy as I was when I was twenty-nine with my first child. Along with my experience in the field there should be no reason why I can't carry a child —and, my OBGYN said I could have one more pregnancy, IF it was my own, meaning not a surrogacy.

Realistically, I know having a child at fifty wasn't the norm, it was not what many fifty- year-olds do. But I wasn't every other fifty-year-old. If not when? What if we could and didn't? What if we could and did? We'd never know unless we tried.

There was no time to waste if we were going to use my eggs. We both got our hopes up. 'Age' at that point to me felt like a four-letter word. I finally settled down, found love, had had babies for other families and I was fairly certain mother nature was going to give me a big fat "NOOOO" to my own eggs, because, hello, I'm 50! The only thing on my side was that my periods were still normal and I was ovulating. I hoped I'd get pregnant naturally, but I knew the odds were most likely not in my favor. Though I held out hope because other women had done it.

There is nothing I can't do if I set my mind to it. My mind flashed back to my mother who told me that all the time, "You can do anything you want in the world, honey, just set your mind to it and go for it."

We had a honeymoon in Australia and soon after that we would start IVF. While in Australia, Paul rented an orange hippy van and we drove, camped, and surfed from Sydney to Cairns plotting out our next moves to create a family. Paul did most of the driving because we were driving on the *wrong side of the road* and I simply could not wrap my brain around it. When we made it to Cairns, we hopped a train and went into the rain forest. It was amazing. The trip was marvelous and one of the best vacations I ever experienced.

I had enough education in the fertility world to know who to go to, but I suspected all those reproductive endocrinologists (IVF Specialists) wouldn't touch a 50-year-old woman without saying the words "egg donation." I knew them pretty well, and sure enough, that is what most of them said.

I googled doctors who had more of an open mind with *older women*. One name kept coming up, Dr. Yanagi. He had started a practice a few years earlier in Irvine, California. I was 45 minutes away.

There was one small thing I thought of later that could be a big thing. I was still unsure of something that might have happened during my C-section surgery with Dr. Raden with regards to our decision to continue with IVF.

Paul and I were having lunch outside one day on a Sunday afternoon and I decided to tell him about my concerns before we proceeded. I was listening more to my intuition and being good to myself.

"Something happened during my flap surgery, the C-section." I said hesitating but wouldn't feel good about proceeding until I knew what happened that day during the surgery." I took another gulp of water.

"What do you mean?" Paul said.

"I was unsure about what Dr. Raden, the Beverly Hills doctor who did the partial tummy tuck which is also referred to as a C-section flap fix, I wasn't sure if he might have done during the surgery.

Paul looked at me reluctantly not knowing what to say. I took a big sigh and continued.

"I had a faint memory of him waking me up during the surgery asking me if I was going to have additional children. Of course, at that moment I said no, because at that time I didn't have plans to have more kids. I simply could not remember the moment as real or exactly what he said, or if it happened at all?

Maybe it was my own thoughts, maybe I thought he woke me up. I was so confused but wanted to make contact with him just in case."

"Before, during and after Dr. Raden and our visits, he never confirmed with me that he had done anything other than what we talked about, and what I signed off on for our agreement to have done. So, I could only assume what I thought happened, didn't happen, but I thought it did." I said.

"Being that I wasn't interested in knowing at that time - I forgot all about it and went on with my business. I didn't think about it again until the accident in August of 2010, right when I met you via computer, strangely enough." I said a little haunted by the timing.

"What happened?" Paul asked as we shared some appetizers. He took another vegetable and dipped it into the garlic hummus.

"Well, I learned via the headline news at 6pm that hot day in August that Dr. Raden accidentally drove off a cliff with his dog in the Malibu Hills while texting. Some reported it wasn't an accident. Many said he was tweeting about his dog the time of the accident. His family claimed it was an accident and he missed the sharp turn and his open jeep and went off the cliff into the rocks below on the beach.

The lifeguards found him down on the rocks below. His dog survived but he did not."

"I tried to reach someone at his office the next day. No one ever returned my ten phone calls that I left messages for and there wasn't anything I could do. Ultimately, I wanted to get my medical records but it was impossible because the office shut down immediately after his death. I couldn't reach anyone. I decided to let it go because I had no need for it then, and I met you."

"Wow, "Paul replied. "Okay, so maybe just in case we can run it by your OBGYNs or something before we do anything?" he said.

"Yes, that'd be wise, just in case." I said. I did really want my records from Dr. Raden's office. I'll check on it again," I said.

I trusted my OBGYN who delivered the majority of the babies I'd given birth to and he put in an order for a structural ultrasound to make sure all was well with me.

I gratefully got the green light to continue when the ultrasound results showed things were totally normal with no known problems, abnormalities, or issues.

Upon visiting Dr. Yanagi's office a month or so later we went through all the paper work and testing, and he took an overall history to assess my fertility. He said I'd be a good candidate, even at fifty years old! He offered to proceed with what is called a natural cycle: Only one egg per month is used, using no fertility drugs and then throughout your cycle you are monitored until the egg retrieval procedure where the doctor takes the egg out of the womb then injects the sperm into the egg in a petri dish using many different medical procedures chosen by the doctor. Certain women were chosen for this procedure due to their own unique circumstances. There are many different types of IVF and each woman is assessed differently due to her age and or her infertility situation or diagnosis.

We went ahead with his protocol five times! And it was a long five months. We were going to stop at four cycles but Dr. Yanagi pushed us ahead and comped one of the cycles because he wanted desperately not only to help us, but make me the oldest patient to be pregnant at fifty years of age with my own eggs. The record holder thus far was forty-eight.

"One more time," Dr. Yanagi said. "One more time. The quality of your embryo is really good for your age."

When the embryologist inserted Paul's sperm into my egg it would multiply normally each time and showed it to be normal until after transfer. Our *maybe baby* made it all the way to transfer each time, but it wouldn't take. Dr. Yanagi inserted it into my uterus with beautiful opera music playing in the background. Then it came time to find out if I was pregnant or not, and every time it was always negative. I was exhausted.

Not pregnant. It fizzled out every time. It was emotionally defeating.

It didn't stick despite the perfect, thick lining in my uterus. After eight long months of infertility treatment, I was done. I'm not sure what part of me gave up first. I think it was ALL of me. I was tired.

We didn't have the beauty of time if I was going to be the one carrying our baby. I was on the other side of the fence with fertility, and had a good idea what all of my intended mothers went through year after year, and how they wanted desperately to be pregnant and could not make a baby without help.

Full Circle for me.

My time had passed for making babies from my DNA. Dr. Yanagi wanted to keep trying. I could not stomach another month of labs, appointments, uterine checks, blood work, shots. I felt it was done, and money was starting to be a factor; this office was much more reasonable than most and I knew well what steps to take to keep the costs down. The money went quick, as always, as little amounts a lot at a time add up fast. Usually, I wasn't so negative but I had a feeling it would not happen no matter how many times I tried.

The only way we could continue would be with an egg donor. We talked about it and decided to go with other avenues like maybe adoption or embryo donation. We both wanted and had a desire to parent together and build a family.

Paul would also often say, "I'm really happy if it's just us, we don't have to do this family thing."

As we moved on, we ran into problem after problem with the different agencies for embryo donation or for adoption and the many places you had to call to get information. We were fighting an uphill battle or not calling or contacting the right places. Most displayed an age requirement policy and wanted younger couples.

After much thought, we decided to move on to egg donation. It took me a while to wrap my head around it because, just like most people, your preference is to use your own genetic material to make a baby.

I contacted an agency I knew who does egg donation. They had thousands of available egg donors. The director was a woman I'd known for a long time through her husband who was an attorney in the surrogacy field. He had drawn up my contract as a surrogate three different times.

We paid a fee and she gave us access to a data base of women who had a desire to be an egg donor. There were young women in college, waitresses, attorneys, you name it. They were all there. Short, tall, all ethnic backgrounds. They all had different reasons to be egg donors. Some knew they never wanted children themselves but wanted to donate their DNA. Others just wanted to help someone else and many wanted both things and more.

Paul sat on one side of the couch in our living room, while I sat on the other, both armed with our laptops. We sat for hours giving thought to what we wanted in our future child and what qualities the egg donor should have based on a five-page question and answer profile with a few pictures of the potential egg donor.

I have to admit that I had a desire for our child to look somewhat like me, but it wasn't mandatory deal-breaker.

We agreed to go through as many as we felt we needed to and come up with our top three choices.

"We both have one that is in our top three." Paul said surprised from the odds.

"Yes, how funny!" I said.

One woman who was in both of our top three, she was the

one we chose. She had never done an egg donation before and was *up in age* for perfect egg donor qualifications. We didn't care: twenty-nine years old was good enough for us. This would be her first egg donation, and our first time using and egg donor.

There is a lot of psychology that comes into play when you can't use your own genetic material vs. using someone else's. I was very sad I wouldn't be able to make a child with the love of my life, but we had choices. *I felt grateful to have a choice.* I had the sense that I knew exactly what some of my intended mothers and women all over the world in this situation might have felt, that we shared the same sadness I was feeling about not being able to have a child with our own genetic material. I felt at one with them, and the ones before them, with all women.

The one thing that helped me the most was I knew we were all inexplicably one, all connected as humans, so it made the process of using an egg donor a much more desirable family choice.

We went through the process and did all of the things we were required to do. There were many steps, and a step by step protocol to be followed exactly. The doctors had it down on all ends.

Dr. Yanagi was ready to do our transfer and rechecked the structural integrity of my uterus. All was cleared and he gave us the official medical go ahead to use Paul's sperm, and the egg from the donor we had chosen.

We didn't know the donor's name or any personal information about her, except she was located in California. However, we did make it abundantly clear in our agreement that IF our child should ever want to contact her, we could contact the agency to connect them: She had notated on her contact information that she would be open to communication at a later date if we, the intended parents, wanted that.

We were going to be open and honest with our future child(ren). I felt particularly strong about that because I didn't meet my biological father until I was nineteen. Your parents, mother and father, will always be your parents but there are biological connections as well.

I was our future child's mother. Paul was our future child's father. We were very fortunate to choose an egg donor who was gracious enough to give a part of herself to make our dreams come true, and help us make a child.

After all was said and done, we ended up with five excellent embryos. Two viable embryos were transferred into me, and three were frozen into cryopreservation for the future.

Upon the initial transfer by Dr. Yanagi, I was pregnant on our first try with an egg donor.

PART TWO

NDE

"The soul is covered by a thousand veils" -Hazrat Inayat Khan

Music: Sleeping at Last – song by Saturn
(lyrics are about the eternal cosmos)

Chapter Sixteen

2013, I'M FIFTY-TWO

Back in the hospital while I was under and my body was lying on the table, I was carefree and on my way to *my heaven*.

Dr. Chen immediately opened my body back up through the same incision he made to take our daughter out of my body. He struggled to find the source of the bleeding as I was still actively bleeding and it needed immediate attention. He proceeded to fill my bladder with saline that was mixed with blue contrast to find the source. According to his surgical notes, there was no evidence of leakage, but I was bleeding somewhere within my body. He couldn't find the cause. He realized he would need help and closed me back up temporarily.

Dr. Chen promptly called an associate, Dr. Mitchell, a specialist in Gynecologic, Oncology, Pelvic Reconstruction Surgery and Advanced Gynecology from a nearby hospital, for an emergency intraoperative consultation. Dr. Mitchell was preparing for surgery at the other hospital, but because my case was such an emergency, he left his patient under anesthesia to come care for me and see what he could do for Dr. Chen. He took over the consultation and upon his assessment, his first concern was my newly sewn up sutures.

"There may be a bladder flap closed in with the sutures.

She's losing blood fast so we have no other option than to open her back up and see if it is the bladder flap." Dr. Chen concurred.

Dr. Mitchell proceeded to open me back up. When he opened the wound and pulled back the abdominal wall, "a significant amount of blood ensued." Then with suction, he "identified a very large torn bladder extending in multiple directions. It was over the dome of the bladder along with multiple adhesions, too many to count."

The strange popping sounds I heard during the C-section when they took our daughter out made sense and were identified by Dr. Mitchell. Somehow, Dr. Chen made a mistake by accidentally obliterating my bladder during childbirth.

In addition to the large tear, Dr. Mitchell found the "bladder flap and the lower anterior part of the bladder had been sewn in with the sutures in closing" by Dr. Chen.

Dr. Mitchell noted, "the closure of the bladder will be very complicated due to the extent of the injury."

By that time, I'd lost a lot of blood and he had to work fast. Dr. Mitchell worked for the next three hours repairing my bladder so that I could use it for the rest of my life.

It was real: the popping sounds during childbirth was my bladder being ripped apart. I was bleeding out internally as a result and was trying to survive "severe postpartum hemorrhage secondary to uterine atony, noted to have extensive abdominal wall and pelvic adhesions."

At that point, per my medical records, I'd lost 2500 ml of blood which is approximately five pints. There are approximately eight pints of blood in an average adult woman and approximately twelve pints in an average adult male.

I soared up into the blue sky. My hair blew back in the gentle breeze. I was leaving earth and into a clearly mystical and unearthly realm.

I was giddy beyond belief. Clouds of white surrounded me as I went through them with my ultra-light and translucent body. I was so excited to be moving on to my next life. Everything was bright and soulful, and something/someone was calling me home. Not like "Susan…" The calling was more than that. The *Om* sound vibrated my knowing, Om, the primordial sound of the Universe. It's a sound that reverberates the entire cosmos in every cell of our bodies. I followed it like I knew where to fly, and I wasn't going to heaven. I was going somewhere else, somewhere *more*.

I processed a thought that I was flying past different divine homes of every spirit in the universe. Every single one I passed in my flight had a far superior intelligence to that of earth and humanity as we know it. The countless higher levels of dimensions were of spirits that have come home to their heavens and they made them up in the stars and exactly how they wanted them.

I was going to join a higher level of angels and I was aware my admission there might be conditional. They were whomever was giving me thoughts telling me these things. Maybe of angels, higher spirits, or dare I say even God? I believed it was my angels. That's it, it was a knowing. They were not voices' in my head, it was a knowing that I knew that they were hesitant to send me there because I might have to return to my body. It might not be my time yet. It was unusual because usually they were sure at this higher level. They waited as I flew to meet them and held space for me to let me come.

However, I also understood that there was an excellent chance I'd be able to stay. I held on to that belief. I was so excited, and believed there was a very high chance I'd be able to stay.

But more than all of that? I was now love, beyond what we know as love here on this planet. The energy of the love was vibrating my being.

L O V E times infinity. I was the love. There was nothing but love, and acceptance, into this realm.

As I flew along to my destination a gentle softness of the starlight around me vibrated and filled me with more divine love. The cosmos was in full view right in front of me. The feeling was like I was being filled up with what I lacked on earth, filled with light and love. I noticed how light I felt without my human body. I knew I left behind my mortal coil, the body on the hospital bed the doctors were trying frantically to save. I never looked back because I knew it was all going to be okay.

While in flight, I tried to touch my arm and it was another form, soft and yielding, not firm. It made me so happy and joyful. I was as light as a feather or maybe even lighter. The energy of it all was a bit overwhelming. I'd touch my arm and go through it from one end to the other with my finger. It was energy matter.

I was interconnected to everything. The stars moved through me like translucent clouds in the sky with no barrier. They moved through every cell in my translucent semi-formed body, and we were one.

I am the stars, and the stars and matter are me.

I was being called, summoned to a place.

The light around me lit up the higher I went. Everything was more illuminating and spectacular.

Time was insignificant. It ceased to exist and I knew it.

This universe was infinite and eternal. I moved up toward the newer, brighter light. The new light was different, a perfect vibrating love. The OM sound vibrated into my body and radiated the ultimate love. The beautiful, serene, magnificent, divine brilliant white light and the stars of magic surrounded me everywhere. I looked around me, the stars so bright, lighting up the darkest parts of the universe and there was love emanating from everything, including me.

As I came to the end of my destination, I can only refer to this place as "my heaven" because that's what everyone might understand. It's a destination, another dimension, and where I stopped along the way. The concept of heaven is something we are all familiar with and one can understand what I'm writing about if I use that term. I believe everyone's version of *heaven* is different.

And, I really have no adequate words to describe what I experienced as this place.

The sound of OMmmmm was so vibrant I could feel it. Bright white light shown everywhere. Was OMmmmm God? I wondered. Was God everything here, all of the energy of the universe?

I looked off in front of me and a little to my left, and there were two circles of angels holding space for me. The smaller circle was inside the larger one, like concentric circles.

Angels! Real live angels were right here and less than fifty feet away from me. I was beyond excited and they were beyond absolutely magnificent. Stunning.

I'm so close, I thought. So close. If I pass this space of circles and join the angels, it will be a new start for me. This was an all-encompassing knowing. It will be what I've dreamed of my whole life, for many, maybe even thousands of lifetimes, something I'd always desired. My life on earth will be done, but I could return if I chose to. It's like all of this was a knowing to me right that moment and something I knew to be true throughout all the lives I've lived. I knew that up here too, and could recall or remember all of the other lives I've lived in the past.

At first glance, all of the angels had *bodies or shapes* of orbed light glowing and radiant with no faces. They had massive white bird-like feathered wings that towered above their orbs and blended into the light. They took away any breath I thought I had left in this realm.

They were divine. They were miraculous. I couldn't stop look-ing, staring at them. I wondered how their wings connected to their faceless orbs of light. Some wore large white robes around the core of their orbed light, their wondrous light. I couldn't tell if they were actually wearing robes or it was attached to their light. The bright white feathered bird-like wings and orbs of light vibrated love and well-being. A thought went through my mind that maybe they wore robes to help my still liminal earthly eyes take in the magnificent light.

"You are loved."

"We were waiting for you." I heard these voices coming into my mind.

The words they said to me were kind, and compassionate words. Voices of no gender told me this straight into my mind, one after another. "You are loved," they said. "You are loved."

It felt like souls talking to each other without words.

The inner circle of angels faced outward and were holding space — praying for me. I don't know how I knew, but they were there for me until the time came that I would join them. They had to hold the space in case I had to return. I could not go past, into, or near the circles of angels until it was time.

The outer circle of angels faced inward with their magnificent wings closing the space inward. They were facing toward each other throughout the circles with their wings on the outside. I was so humbled and in awe of their bird-like wings towering over their orbed light tops. All I heard was the vibration of OM, softly, then medium-loud, and then so loud I wanted to melt into my own being and join the vibration. At least a dozen angels were in each of the two circles.

The light was so bright I squinted my eyes tightly, then tried so hard to stare but would have to look away or shield my eyes with my hands every so often. I peeked through my fingers because it was so overwhelmingly brilliant and bright love light.

Two concentric circles of angelic angels, what does it mean? And why were they faced the way they were? It was so unusual. I'd never seen anything like it, even in pictures. I moved over to the side where the light was a tiny bit dimmer. I waited expectantly, standing there with excitement in my hospital gown. I was so excited to move on.

I understood without anyone speaking that this gathering

was important because it would determine whether I stay or go back to earth. There was a very high chance that I was going to be able to move on, to become an angel, one of these angels. I desperately wanted to stay.

It was clear to me that I died and left my loved ones on earth. I was a free soul who loved unconditionally and my death was beautiful. On earth we lost people and we mourned because that is the way it's done there with feelings. Here it was only to celebrate love and home.

I was in the here and now, right now with this moment - - but not in time.

I had an understanding that being on earth was for all of us to learn and individually grow into love, and to know oneself. Every single person on earth was doing the same thing: we were there to learn and grow with feelings. Here we were beings in love. I felt every human being on earth, every soul connected to me, not just my family, but everyone. I understood the angels watched over everyone and closely monitored souls on earth learning and growing, moving in and out of space and time.

I would have a thought and then a confirmation of what I was thinking would be voiced: "We are all connected," I heard in the most divine voice.

I knew my family would be fine, and I would see them again someday and we would connect as souls on a journey at some point in time. Some souls on earth I've felt an incredible connection to, and to others, not so much. In my heaven you know those souls and you connect on a different level.

I continued to watch the angels, and the sound of OM was at a low pitch again and getting louder by the moment. It would get really loud and then go back down to a low pitch. The sound vibrated into total bliss, like rings radiating out through a rippling pond, here with sound and vibration. I wanted to be with them, to join them.

I knew if I moved on to my heaven, it would be to a *higher-level angel position* that was a magnificent one, and one I'd

always wanted, one of divine intervention. I had an unbelievable thought that all of this was supposed to happen. It was all
predetermined.

I didn't question the *levels* of angels at the time of my
journey, but I did when I returned. I didn't want to believe
that *levels* existed in a perfect heaven but I could never find a
word to suffice and explain it. I would find later that there were
Hierarchy of Angels, and the highest angel was a Seraphim,
angels of love, light and guardians of God's throne and found a
quote that fit my journey.

"The entire hierarchy of angels can best be described as an
endlessly vast sphere of beings, who surround an unknowable
center point, which is called God." - Malcolm Godwin

Every moment of my life up to this time, all that has ever
happened to me, felt planned. Every choice I ever made up
to this point was my reality and what I made it. I was beyond
excited. It was time.

Everything was divine, I was loved. Loved beyond
expression.

I had a knowing again that I spent numerous lifetimes on
earth. This reincarnation would be different and that was why
it felt so special. I would have the opportunity to say whether
or not I wanted to return to earth again. I'd become an orbed
light angel and learned more lessons than I'd ever thought I'd
learn in a lifetime. I would help others achieve a higher realm
of understanding.

I was *home.*

As I glanced up again, I was having a hard time containing
my excitement. My eyes were fixed on one of the angels in
the inner circle. One light orbed-faced angel turned around
in the inner circle as I stared. The face slowly transformed
into the face of Jesus. I recognized his face. He raised his left
hand slowly, gently, his arm reaching out. The whole of his
body transformed as his giant white robe hung low over what
appeared to be his hand, the hand of a human. His upper body

looked *human*, and I stood breathless staring at him in awe. Although this one particular orbed light angel now looked human, he felt my excitement. He pointed one finger up and said to me via telepathy, in a calm deep and reassuring voice, "Be Still."

I calmed down immediately and felt the space around me full of love.

He conveyed the message because the Jesus angel knew I was eager to move on. Maybe he knew I'd wanted so badly to cross the circles and he needed to catch my attention with the two most important words I'd ever hear spoken in my life, *be still.*

This was directly from Jesus! But wait, I was confused because I wasn't religious. I was much more spiritual than religious.

"Why Jesus?" I thought to myself.

I was a girl who doubted a lot of things, and took a very long time to trust anyone or anything in this life I've lived up until now. I didn't believe in religion and didn't want any religious people or books telling me what I could or couldn't believe in, or what was right or wrong. What did all of it really mean?

In this moment, I was experiencing *my heaven.* I believed God was in nature, in me and in you, and every living thing. God was energy. I was spiritual, not religious. In the past few years of my life I'd come to not believe in the make-believe man up in the sky, but there he, *it,* the angel was — the face of Jesus, the bright light orb of Jesus. *What was happening? What did it mean?*

I couldn't believe I was looking at the face of Jesus, and questioned it as I stood watching the transformation right before my eyes. It kept getting crisp and clearer. It was the face of Jesus. *What does this mean?* I thought again and stared.

After the second wondering of what it all meant, within my mind I had the answer instantly from the collective knowledge of angels I was surrounded by.

A knowing came over me that religion does not divide us. It is supposed to *connect* us. We have spiritual teachers like Jesus, and there are religious beliefs, and we are on earth to support one another and move along and learn lessons we need to be able to move on to another life. We simply shift states of being, it doesn't mean that it ends. It means there is a new reality to participate in.

It is also true for every human on earth. When it is their time, they come home too.

"*Christ Consciousness is your teacher,*" another voice said. The kind of teacher who knows what you're going through, where you've been, where you're going, and guides you into your own being. They don't make choices for you. They know you intimately inside and out and strive for the alignment of your soul, and are with you always.

I saw that religion was for spiritual teaching, and no matter how you believed, or what you believed, or even if you didn't believe at all, that you were a part of the energy of God., inside to the core of your human body, the spirit of your consciousness, and every living cell of your body, connected like the stars and matter in the sky. It was like the universe was one big living organism, all of us connected. Every leaf, tree and flower on earth that roots out finding ways to grow, and looks like branches in the lungs inside your body was connected to the Omniscient, Omnipotent, God.

God wasn't some made up person in the sky. God was the energy of every living thing. *YES*, I thought, that is what I believed.

This made a humongous difference for me. I had never been able to articulate it like this knowing I received in *my heaven*. It had never been confirmed from all the searching I did into different types of religion, and I had eventually given up.

Jesus' face represented my teacher and all of the other spiritual beings and enlightened teachers helping us all walk home together again.

I absorbed everything in that short time that I'd been searching for all of my life, and everything I needed was right inside me.

I learned I was God and God was me. If you want to call God energy, that's what I believed before I came here. It meant the energy and life force on earth and in space, the planets, the stars, everything else in nature was all connected inside of me. I didn't need anything else outside of myself to be whole.

The first time I said this sort of thing to myself years before I thought it was kind of woo-woo, and I felt kind of fake comparing myself to God, or saying I was God or God was me. It took a lot of time to try it on. Many people don't understand this concept in elementary terms. When it's used in an energy way, it doesn't mean that I think I am God, like the 'man in the sky.' It means that the energy of God flows through me and in me. That's it. I think it's different for each and every one of us, and I know I am not the first one to express this concept.

This experience was beyond my realm of thinking and I had no words, no real vocabulary to express the pure and utter beauty, love, and feelings I had while out of my human body.

Was it consciousness itself or was it my consciousness? Perhaps my soul? Were they all connected as spirit? Maybe it does exist outside of time and space? How does consciousness connect? Is my soul also my consciousness? Is this the big picture or part of the big picture? I was full of questions.

Physics or quantum physics can't explain it, no one can. I'm certain it is of the magical, spiritual world and will remain a mystery so everything can continue on exactly how the spiritual world has always existed.

I knew intuitively the universe must be huge, so this was just a little part of the whole.

I thought to myself and stood in awe watching something that was totally blowing my mind, and at the same time, I knew it to be exactly what my destiny was and what I belonged to, and where I wanted to be.

Back under on the surgery table, the only way Dr. Mitchell could save my life was to do a total reconstruction of my bladder. I learned Dr. Mitchell been called over several times in the past by Dr. Chen and it was always a consultation that required fifteen to thirty minutes of his time. Not this time. To save my life he would work on me for nearly five hours.

Hours after my bladder was repaired, Dr. Mitchell was ready to return to the other hospital. He'd contained the bleeding enough to be done with this part of the surgery. It was noted at that time that I was still bleeding and would require a partial hysterectomy. My uterus was weeping blood, not able to return to its original form. The muscles had given out and wouldn't hold form.

Dr. Chen went to the nursery where Paul was feeding our daughter to obtain authorization to take out part of my womb.

"We are going to have to take part of Susan's uterus, at least the part of it that won't stop bleeding," he said taking half breaths, exhausted. "Dr. Mitchell has completed the reconstruction of Susan's bladder and the team has decided it's in Susan's best interest to do a partial hysterectomy. It is still bleeding. We need your consent before we continue. She's lost more blood, approximately 500 ml."

"So, she'll never be able to get pregnant again?"

"No," Dr. Chen confirmed.

Paul didn't hesitate to give the authorization, but added, "You are going to have to tell Susan, Dr. Chen. You are going to have to tell her that you had to take her uterus."

Dr. Chen's surgical cap was drenched with sweat. Paul said he nodded and looked defeated, exhausted and out of energy as he left the room to go back to the operating room.

Doctors were going in and out of the room meeting with Paul while he was feeding our daughter. Paul mentioned that all of the doctors were working together to save my life, they all looked exhausted and emotionally torn as they worked on me throughout the day.

"Nothing like this has ever happened in my career. Nothing like this," Dr. Chen said to Paul wiping his brow as he left the nursery to return to the emergency room.

As the surgery progressed, Dr. Chen updated Paul every so often. Paul was going back and forth to the nursery to help care for our daughter. The hospital was starting to phase out nurseries and not make them available any longer. All babies were to room in with the parents. They had a few nurses available until the change took place. This meant Paul would have to learn quickly how to take care of our daughter.

No one, including our family and friends, knew what was happening. No one knew we were having a baby. We didn't have time to alert everyone because we didn't know if we'd stay.

Then Paul started to realized that he would have to tell me that my uterus, my sacred body part was now cut in half, right across the middle. He wasn't sure if Dr. Chen would do it or if he would see me first, but he knew what it meant to me. A body part that I'd used well, one I would not be able to use again. He knew I might not take it well to learn I was now infertile.

Giving life gave me life. Paul knew how precious it was to me.

Though I never got the message of being done having children, the choice was made for me, to save my life.

I'd gone full circle without ever intending to, from being a mother and surrogate mother to being infertile. I would see how the grass was not greener on the other side of the fertility fence.

Just before Dr. Mitchell left for his patient in the other hospital, he called in one of his associates, Dr. Adams, for emergency assistance to "ensure that the superacervical hysterectomy was done in the proper way to avoid any potential complication from the incidental cystotomy."

Which meant he wanted to keep the bladder intact and install a leg Foley catheter to the bladder. Dr. Adams would do the partial hysterectomy which meant only taking out the part that was bleeding by basically cutting the womb in half but leaving everything else in place. He would also install the 3-way Foley catheter that I would have to wear on my leg for urine output for four to six weeks postpartum depending on my condition and IF the surgery worked, and depending on how the bladder held up as time went on. Otherwise I would have to wear a catheter for urine output for the rest of my life.

Dr. Mitchell had told Paul honestly before the surgery, "I'm not sure this is going to work. I've never done a complete bladder reconstruction before. Like ever." He'd been an OBGYN surgeon for over twenty-two years.

Dr. Adams worked his magic. I was finally stable and not bleeding.

They ordered blood for me. It was noted in my medical files that I received "three units of packed red blood cells and four units of fresh frozen plasma for hemostasis." A normal woman has nine units at any given time in her adult life, I required seven units to live, to come back to life.

I have a whole new perspective on people who give blood and now regularly, routinely give blood whenever I can, to give back.

Thank you from the bottom of my heart to all the blood and life givers.

Love was the message, and I was there to receive it. I wish a thousand wishes every day that I could wave a wand and let you know how it actually *feels*. Then you'd know.

Upon my return, I was so frustrated because the NDE, near-death-experience was so hard to explain to those I loved. I can still tap into it when I meditate or when I'm still. I remember everything.

Honestly, sometimes I want to go back, even now, but I know what that means. I'm here for now until I learn more of what I need to learn, and when I have, I will return. Will what I experienced still be my same reality? I have no idea, and I don't believe it matters because it's all love. I'm reminded of this love every single day of my life. I think about it all the time.

It's *beyond* unconditional love, its pure and powerful love. There is nothing questioned with this kind of love, it just is.

If you've lost someone you've loved in your life, a person that maybe you are still in grief about losing regardless of who they are, know they are in and surrounded by the most beautiful, magnificent love. It's the basis and foundation of the theory of everything. Your loved one's light spirits are moving on, and want you to live your life when you are ready, and live it with love and meaning. You might even connect with them again someday.

Back In my heaven, the Om sounds became a part of me, of my being. It felt like I was standing while I was waiting but felt like floating at the same time. The primordial universal music of OM... I was calm, remembering the words from Jesus to me, "Be Still."

Being still brought me to a new understanding. The sound of music, "OM..." calmed me. "Be still" I was grateful for the knowing.

The illuminated light became so bright I had to turn my head away. I took my hands and covered my eyes.

I started to get confused. "Wait," I said either in my mind or out loud. "I want to stay."

I heard multiple voices filling my mind saying, "It's not your time. You have more to do." The voices echoed in my mind.

I thought, "no, wait... what?!" I remained confused, wanting to move on and join my two circles of light orbed angels.

Full Circle Angels.

The voices muffled at different times, several voices filling my mind, my being came in taking over and echoed the same words again as I felt myself go back.

But this time I didn't fly.

It was an abrupt, harsh and fast return into my mangled cut up, sewn up human body. I believe what I felt was the liminal darkness of matter and the separational invisible divide upon my return.

Many people who will pick up this book will not know me personally. Anyone who has ever known me, knows I am not someone to tell or share made-up stories or lie about something as important as this. This is information I received on my journey from *my heaven* that I know I must share.

After it happened and at first, I felt silly for telling everyone I knew about my experience, and sometimes I still do. Most importantly those in my close circle of love do believe me. I was never a teller of lies and now I know what death is, and what it might look like when the final end comes. It has changed my every day normal life drastically.

The pure beauty of it all is that I no longer care what others think about me because they didn't come with me on my journey, and I know, in my heart of hearts, what happened to me was real, as real as the nose on my face.

The fact that I came back to earth with absolutely no fear of death has stayed with me to this day. The awareness of my experience was, and into itself, a perfect piece of *my heaven*. The memory of it came back with me! The remembering of my experience is still crystal clear to this day.

Perhaps, zero fear about death was the biggest gift I could have ever received during this journey. It helps me live my life bigger. A more amazing thing to share is the absence of fear regarding death to everyone I know, and everyone I don't know.

I opened my eyes in the ICU on July 3rd, 2019.

PART THREE

AFTER

"All endings are also beginnings.
We just don't know it yet." – Mitch Albom

Music: Jason Mraz – Love Is Still the Answer
(love, the only answer)

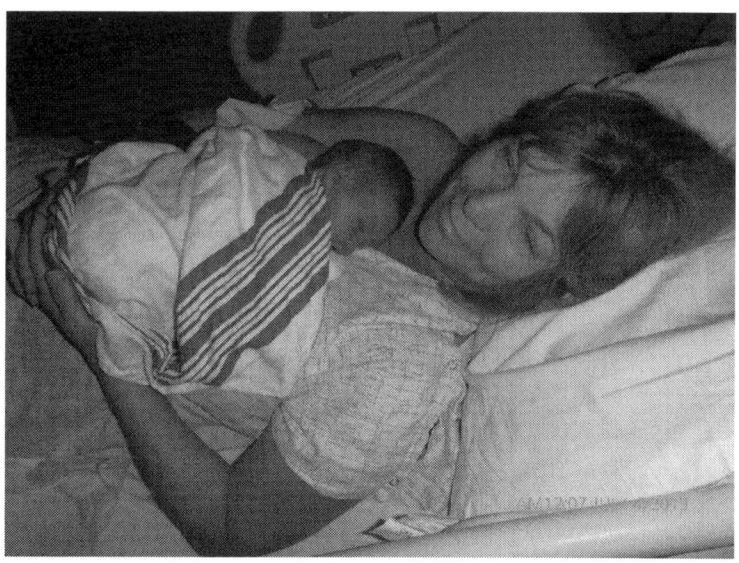

Chapter Seventeen

The moment I opened my eyes, big awareness went to my entire body feeling incredibly heavy. I tried to lift my head, not knowing where I was. It came up a little bit and I looked around. I knew I was back on earth. Everything felt different. Confined.

Tears started rolling down the sides of my face. The memory of my journey was so vivid, colorful, and remained in my mind; flashes of light here and there and flashes of my journey were popping up in my mind. The moment I knew I was coming back, my mind was saying, "I want to stay, please let me stay." It was so peaceful and loving there.

Then the guilt found a way to sneak into my thoughts, then it washed over my whole body. I wanted to stay there, where I went out of my body instead of being here. That wish made it feel like I was leaving my family on purpose.

Guilt.

While in *my heaven*, I knew my family was going to be all right. Although they would miss me when I was gone, I knew it would all be okay because all of us souls were on our endless journeys. On my journey it was all perfectly okay, here on earth it was different. The guilt would continue to confound me and was part of the heaviness in my heart and body. I was so confused. I knew I wouldn't be confused in my heaven. I felt guilt here, but not in *my heaven.*

I was attached to a lot of machines and plastic bags hung above my head. I looked over at a nurse hooking up the plastic lines that went into me; she was putting up another bag of blood. *A bag of blood?* I thought. *For me? What happened?* I'd never been given blood before.

I heard a female voice say, "I'm getting a room together for you. We're moving you out of ICU right now, but you still have two units of blood to take in so we'll move those with you."

What? I thought. She jerked the bed hard to get it moving and my head felt dizzy. She pushed up the arms of the bed and started to wheel me down the corridor.

I couldn't move. My body felt heavy like concrete, like it was thicker than before, greater in density. I looked at all the tubes running into my arms, and had no strength to lift them. Her words were loud, too loud for my ears. *Be quiet,* I thought. *Please be quiet.*

The nurse reached for the bags over my head. There were a lot of intravenous drip bags above me, maybe five or more bags of fluid. Two of them held dark, carmine blood. I'd never had a blood transfusion so this was completely new to me.

She adjusted all of the bags to make sure they were working properly. When she finished, she leaned into me on my right side and said in a hushed whisper, "*Don't forget what I am saying to you.*" She moved in so close to me, her lips right at my ear, I could feel her warm breath as she said, "*What they did to you was just plain wrong.*"

I was more confused. I remembered being in the hospital having a baby, then having an amazing experience, and now, I was just waking up. I knew I gave birth to my daughter, and then something happened. *What happened? Where is our little girl? Where is my husband?* I thought but didn't say out loud.

There were no immediate answers like there were in my heaven.

I don't remember what the nurse looked like but I remembered her being very fresh smelling like a rich, earthy vanilla and amber soap.

I moaned at the heaviness of my body when I tried to move to a comfortable position. Everything hurt. I felt so leaden but knew deep inside of the extreme love hovering just above me, remembering when I touched the energy of my formless body just a little big ago.

A thought came into my mind: The circles. The circles of angels. What did it mean? I waited for answers but none came.

I'd always been fascinated with circles but this time the full circle represented my life. In the past, I've noticed the shape of circles in my life and pointed them out often. A perfect embryo is a sphere that grows and transforms into a baby. The planets in the solar system, the sun and the moons. A circle never ends.

A very tall, handsome man with wavy, dark brown hair over his ears came into my room wearing a white doctor's coat. I stared at him, but my brain didn't recognize him. Everything was a bit blurry. I rubbed my eyes.

"Hello there, I'm Dr. Mitchell." As he walked toward me, I saw his warm, sweet smile. He reached for my hand with an open palm, and I instinctively put my arm out to place my hand in his. "We're so glad you made it," he said. "I helped reconstruct your bladder."

I nodded, feeling shaky, weak and loopy while I sent out invisible vibes of love to him. I thought I should say something, say thank you but for some reason couldn't find the words. I didn't know this man, yet I felt he was the most caring, gentle doctor who ever lived.

"Thank you." I managed in the softest most grateful voice.

"You're welcome." He said.

I felt instantly lucky, but then I thought about my experience, the journey I went on which was still very vivid, clear and colorful in my mind, and at that moment I wasn't sure if I was *lucky* or not.

I could sense that he had somewhere else he had to go in a hurry, but he'd made time to stop by and see me before he had to leave. As he turned to leave the room, he let go of my hand and then grabbed my foot, softly reassuring me, "You're going to be just fine.".

I wanted to cry.

I did not know then that he was the one who saved my life, my guardian angel. I barely remembered seeing him, and I'm not sure when he came to see me but know I saw him, before I saw Paul.

Dr. Chen had kept Paul updated every so often, and other people came to help all of us. Taking care of a newborn was all new for Paul. At that time, the head nurse helped him because the staff was low due to the holiday and because she was informed about our situation. My medical needs meant Paul would have to learn quickly how to take care of our daughter. She gave him years of wisdom in a few short hours.

"Hi," Paul said gently, warmly and sweetly when he came in and stood by my side. He wasn't holding our daughter.

"Our daughter is feeding right now with the nurse so I can see you. She has quite an appetite." he said. "She is healthy and doing fine."

"Hi," I said to him softly.

"Baby, I'm so glad you're here, with us."

"Me too," I said with tears welling up in my eyes. Paul hugged me and kissed my lips with so much love. He pulled a chair over to my bedside to sit close to me. He looked sad, and happy — bittersweet. He had something serious to tell me. I looked at him intently.

At that point, I learned later, he didn't know if Dr. Chen told me or not so he took it upon himself to give me the news.

"Honey. Susan. They had to take part of your womb to save your life, and I gave them permission to do it."

As I tried to sit up and take it all in, Paul's words hit me like a ton of bricks. My head fell back onto the pillows. I wanted to hide my face and disappear into nothingness, and I'm sure my face showed exactly what I was thinking. I was shocked and I instantly started crying. Tears streamed from my eyes. I knew what this meant.

I still didn't know exactly what had happened to me and I didn't know what to say. I felt good that I'd used my womb, my uterus, well. *I would not be able to use it again in this lifetime. Ever.*

The finality struck me.

"I haven't called anyone yet. I didn't know what to say to everyone until we knew more," Paul said as tears started falling down his face.

"It's okay," I said between my sniffles. "I used it well."

I reached out my hand, and he leaned in and hugged me with such strength, so warm and deep. We cried together.

"Call them all, the boys first, then my sister and brothers, and Terrie," I said, wiping away my tears. Let them know about how we all are, and that I'm still here." We both realized at that moment that no one knew we were having a baby because we didn't know ourselves until the previous morning.

"You've been in the ICU since late afternoon and overnight after the birth," and then he proceeded to tell me everything. I just listened, not really taking it all in. My mind kept going back into the clouds and I kept thinking about my journey, trying to distinguish the difference between what I had seen and reality on earth. How in the world was I going to tell him about all I saw during the time between when I died and came back? What would he say, and would he believe me? *Did it really happen?* I started to doubt myself. *The angels*, I thought. *Those magnificent wings.*

Paul stayed with me for about an hour. He mentioned that he hadn't eaten for a long while.

"I'm going to grab a quick bite and then I'll be back soon."
I wasn't ready to tell him yet. *Maybe later*, I thought.
"Okay. I love you." I said in a whisper.
"I love you, too, so very much," he said, and turned toward the hospital door.

I quickly fell asleep and started to dream.

I was alone walking barefoot in my hospital gown in a forest and could hear a stream nearby. I followed the sound and when I got to the stream it looked just like the stream I sat by as a child when I hid away from the world. It was so colorful with all the flowers of the rainbow, with the green of the grass greener than any green I've seen before. Tall grass and leaves crumbling and crunching under my bare foot. I listened to the stream, and it calmed me as water often does. The air was so clean, like the tops of mountains and smell clean air that only mountains can provide.

In that moment, I realized I was a tree hugging, flower sniffing mammal, and I loved nature, the dirt, and I considered everything beautiful. I knew I could meld into the landscape and stay forever.

I awoke from the dream knowing it was only a dream knowing it wasn't anything like my NDE.

It reminded me of a saying from Thich Nhat Hahn's book, *No Death, No Fear: Comforting Wisdom for Life. Hahn* is a Vietnamese Buddhist monk and peace activist. He is 93 and miraculously still alive (as of this writing) even after numerous strokes. He said:

"When conditions are sufficient things manifest. When conditions are no longer sufficient things withdraw. They wait until the moment is right for them to manifest again." To me it meant that nature is born and reborn again and again, and so are we as humans.

Paul got back from lunch and said he'd made all the calls to our family to update them and announce our daughter's birth.

Steven had been in Mexico on vacation when I was in the hospital, and I wouldn't see him until I got home five days later. Brian came to the hospital as fast as he could, and I could see the worry on his face when he came to see me. I hugged him tight and said, "It's all okay, I'm okay and here for a long time."

"Terrie is well and working. She'll be in as soon as she can."

I nodded, happy to think of my dear friend.

"So, are we going with the original name we chose for our daughter?" Paul asked as he took a seat on the uncomfortable chair he had slept on the night before.

I said, "I love the name, baby, but I hesitate because you know it's hard to pronounce and people just freak out about different names. And she'll always be correcting people." I noticed how much better I felt after my nap. I still felt heavy but not as heavy as before.

"Who cares," Paul said. "She's unique and she came here for a reason. Her name will be different. Her family and friends will know and speak her name clearly and always remember it."

"Yeah, that's true," I said. I was pretty sure I wasn't going to change his mind. He loved the name: Nevaeh.

We had sat around one night before we got pregnant talking about naming our future child and *Nevaeh* came up a few times as a girl's name during his research on good, unique, spiritual and meaningful names. This name, Nevaeh, went back centuries and came up several times in Paul's search in *The Triangular Book*. It is a book of Count Saint Germain's time and it is listed as the password to get into heaven: Heaven backwards is N E V A E H.

The sudden surprise hit me. I opened my mouth instinctively and put my hand over it. With joyful tears I realized it was heaven, spelled backwards!

We planned to pronounce it with two syllables, *Nah vay*. The original pronunciation is with three syllables, *Nah-vay-ah*.

Back then we looked at each other and toasted in the air with our wine glasses. "Nevaeh!" (Nah-vay) we said together.

After I took a sip of wine I added "but let's wait until we see the faces of our children to name them, okay?" He agreed.

"Honey," I said quietly to Paul. "I saw angels, like real live angels." He looked at me in surprise trying to discern what I said.

"What?" he asked.

"Angels. I saw angels and I was out of my body and somewhere else in the universe."

He sat up in the chair and directly looked at me.

"I saw angels in the foyer of the hospital!" he said in amazement to me. "I wasn't going to say anything because I wasn't sure you'd believe it. They were at the opening of the hospital entrance lined up all the way to your room when I got back from lunch."

"You saw the ones I saw?" I said confused. Tears falling down my face.

"I don't know, what'd you see?" he asked.

I proceeded to tell him everything I experienced with the full depth of my emotions exposed because I couldn't tell the story without sobbing.

He was speechless when I was done but did say, "Wow, that's a lot more than just seeing angels lined up against the wall." He said with an utter astonishment and wonder.

"What did your angels look like?" I asked. I listened with the excitement of this all being so surreal, almost unbelievable.

"They were off white, like beige with wings. All the same color. They knew I could see them and it felt to me like they were guardian angels for you. There was no particular form, just what I would consider light energy. It was almost a static energy of angelic form. Like if I put my hand out it'd go right through them."

We both looked at each other awestruck at what we had each experienced, witnessing each other and reveling in the beautiful fact we could talk openly to each other about anything and be comfortable.

"Nevaeh it is. Heaven spelled backwards. The closest to heaven," Paul sat back in his chair.

"Yes," I said, "yes, Nevaeh."

"I'll go get Nevaeh and bring her in here with us."

I smiled and nodded.

He might as well of said he was bringing heaven to be with us on earth.

We spent July 4th 2013 in the hospital, all three of us getting used to each other. I was recovering and starting to remember more. I was able to walk and get around a little by then but still felt so heavy. So damn heavy. Guilt popped up here and there. Guilt about having wanted to leave my family and stay in my heaven. I was sure it was part of the human heaviness I was carrying on this earth. *Why did I have to bring this back?* I thought. *Anyone would have chosen heaven instead.*

At the time I got back to my house, I believe I was still in a fog. It would take time for me to feel better and I was grateful Paul was home for a few weeks to help me. I wore the bladder bag (what they call a purse) on my thigh, and I had to learn how to drain it every few hours. My C-section scar was healing. I felt a little bit depressed, but and was probably still confused. I decided to give myself a lot of time. One. Day. At. A. Time.

Once I was more steadily up and about at home, Steven came to visit and hold his little sister.

"Nevaeh has red hair!" he said, delighted and surprised.

It was so good to see him, hug him, and tell him I loved him.

"Jesus, you scared me, Mom. I love you," he said. We hugged. I cried some more. I could tell I did scare him because of the look on his face. It reminded me of his little boy face when he was really young and would get scared occasionally. As I looked at this young man all grown up, I smiled inside knowing he'd always be my little boy.

This news about me came out of nowhere for him. Nothing that happened recently was on his or anyone's radar. He wasn't sure how to process it, and I wasn't able to throw in my NDE information yet, but I would tell him when the time was right and it was just us two.

"So, how do you say her name again?" he said, holding Nevaeh to his chest while she slept soundly.

A few weeks later I invited Brian to breakfast so we could talk and I could share my NDE with him. I felt a need to share it with those closest to me, I needed for them to know. I wasn't sure what words to use. It would be my first public telling of my NDE after telling Paul. I wanted to tell Brian and Steven because I wanted them to know what happened to me, this profound experience, directly from me.

I was a little afraid they wouldn't believe me, but regardless I was ready to put my vulnerability out there. I felt it was so important and hoped it might pave the way for them to explore their own beliefs.

I started to talk right before our breakfast of eggs and pancakes with bacon was served. I told Brian the whole story.

"Mom... what?" he asked, puzzled, fiddling around with his scrambled eggs.

I nodded. "It's all true and I can't explain it better than I just did, and I can't get someone to confirm it." He looked into my eyes to really connect with me and know I was telling him the truth. "It wasn't a dream, Bri. It was real. You know me well enough to know I would never make up something like this."

He looked at me again. Deeper. I thought he might be looking for some kind of meaning for himself.

I could tell he believed me, but was still a little skeptical about it, and that was okay. I thought about people I loved telling me exactly what I just told Brian and I thought maybe I might react that way, too. Grasping, for something, anything to make sense of an outrageous story.

If I only did one positive thing with this experience, I created the opportunity for growth into his mindset for an expanded worldview that included a new possibility and maybe purpose of spirituality, and an unlimited universe. That was plenty in just one conversation with his mother. Someone he trusted. I knew it was going to take some time for him to absorb it all.

When I told Steven, he reacted almost the exact same way, and again I saw it was definitely going to take time.

They were still getting over the fact that their mother almost died.

Chapter Eighteen

2013, I'M STILL FIFTY-TWO

Six weeks after our daughter Nevaeh was born, and I was still recovering from the momentous events of that day, I had a yearning to visit Dr. Mitchell, the man who saved my life. I felt compelled to thank him so I made an appointment to see him.

His waiting room was packed with mostly women sitting on a small square of couches. Every single seat was occupied except for a small bit of a couch, just barely enough for me to sit with Nevaeh in the carrier at my feet. Paul stood up by the reception desk where two other men were, likely there for support as well. The lady next to me smiled as I sat and peered at our baby, looking first at me and then at Paul.

"Oh my God, look at her red hairs" she said. We heard that often because she did have more and more short crimson hair strands coming out on her sweet head. She was definitely going to be a redhead.

When I made the appointment, I made it clear that I just wanted to see the doctor for a quick short visit. They must have slipped me in because the room was busy in this OBGYN oncologist's office. It struck me oddly that I'd be in an oncology office if I didn't have cancer.

One older lady in particular, with pretty silver hair, stared at me, smiling from across the small room as I rocked our daughter in her carrier. I smiled back. It was the kind of smile that conveyed sweetness and wisdom and an acknowledgment. *You are so very lucky to have such a healthy young baby. I wonder why you're here?* Do we all wonder these things? I know I have. *God,* I thought, *if she only knew I wouldn't be here if it weren't for her doctor.*

I wanted to bring big thank you balloons or cupcakes, cookies, or something. I wanted to shout it from the mountaintops that life is good, heaven is beautiful, and we're all so lucky to be here to learn, love, and go back home and start all over again the next day. I was sure I would make a fool of myself, though. Given that my family had a hard time taking in my NDE, I'd probably end up feeling very embarrassed. So, of course, I didn't do it. Bringing cookies or snacks or something would have probably overwhelmed the office, the front for sure. I didn't know what to do or how much to bring, so I just made it a regular office visit.

We were called back and I walked into a large room with big machines filling the back of the room. Paul walked in behind me holding Nevaeh. I saw Dr. Mitchell half way across the room and headed straight for him to give him probably the biggest hug I've ever given anyone. It was a hug of huge gratitude. "Thank you, Dr. Mitchell," I said as tears rolled down my cheeks. I looked at him as we finished hugging. He had the softest brown eyes.

"You're so welcome," he said, this time giving me a hug. It felt like he was so happy that he could help and that it all turned out so well. He went above and beyond, put passion into his work and clearly valued emotional connections.

After we hugged, I looked back at Paul who had put Nevaeh back into the carrier, and he came over and hugged Dr. Mitchell, too. It was such a beautiful moment. I was so grateful. "Thank you, doctor, he said tearfully. "Our family is complete."

"You welcome. So very welcome," Dr. Mitchell said humbly.

"How is the bladder working Susan?" the doctor asked interested.

My bladder was on the way to being restored and I had an appointment in two weeks to make sure it could hold liquid and not be compromised or leak. If there was no leakage, I could get the Foley bag off my thigh, and finally let my bladder work on its own. I could not wait for that day. I hated the bag and having to change it three to four times a day.

"So far, so good. I can't wait to get the purse off my leg though," I said touching my leg. "I hope the bladder can do its thing."

"Me too, me too. It was all new and if you haven't had problems so far it should be just fine."

It made me feel a lot better. We talked a bit more and he proceeded to tell me about my condition and what he did for me six weeks before.

"When I got to you, your bladder was as flat as a pancake" He took his palm and flattened it face up. Then he cupped his hand into a fist and said, "It needed to look like this as a bladder," showing Paul and me the significant difference. "So, I took it in my hands and cupped it up gently. My team of three at first, then seven, assisted me to restore life to your bladder by sewing it all up to make sure it would have room to heal on its own. In the medical world, it's officially called a bladder reconstruction."

I'm so glad I followed my instinct in wanting to thank him in person. I'll never forget that appointment with him, and him taking time to see me in between his patients. He mentioned toward the end of our visit, "most of my patients have cancer and don't always have a bright outlook, so it was a pleasure to help someone like you make it and carry on with a new family." He smiled broadly.

I'm sure I said "thank you" a hundred times more and knew it still would never be enough for what he did for me.

I told him the short version of my NDE experience and

he said he'd had patients who had also had them. He believed in it, and said he'd leave it to the experts, meaning the people who've had them, and the "conscious spiritual explorers."

The next day I went to the hospital to get my medical records. I wanted to know exactly what happened while I was in surgery. It was all so much to process.

There was still a little part of me that doubted what I experienced during my brief death and return to life. I kept wondering if it was something in my brain that 'fired off' or maybe something based in brain science that I didn't understand about consciousness. That little doubt was enough to stop the new exciting spiritual journey I was on, and it was enough to make me doubt everything I knew to be true.

One of the biggest questions I had was about the circles. What was their significance? Why were the angels facing the way they were? I sought out answers online backward, forward and sideways to no avail. Google had no answers for me after hours and hours in a year of internet deep diving.

It would take another five years to read the 75 pages of the medical report then actually digest it all and break it out into sections so I could understand the complex notes. I was fairly sure they wanted it to be unreadable and not be understandable.

Many people asked if we sued the doctor or the hospital, and we did not. I felt happy to be alive and grateful to Dr. Mitchell for saving my life. For the longest time I would say, "Why would I sue a place, or a doctor that gave me the best experience of my life?" That is how I felt about my NDE journey. It was something special and something I was slowly building on to understand more about.

Weeks later, I sat on a plastic seat in the waiting room of an outpatient hospital. I went to the hospital to see if my bladder was holding up properly and there was no leakage. Dr. Mitchell had a standing order for me to make sure the reconstruction of my bladder was a success. I went the first day I was cleared to go. I wanted so badly to get the bladder purse off my leg, and I was afraid that it might not be healed. I did not want to wear this thing on my leg forever.

Fear took over my body and I started to shake uncontrollably.

"Please step up onto the big wheel," the tech said. I looked at her like she might be a little crazy: It looked like after I stepped up there, they would just spin me round and round.

It resembled and was as big as the wheel on The Wheel of Fortune, the famous gameshow. All of a sudden to me, it was a wheel of luck. I wasn't so sure I was going to win everything or anything. Lucky? Unlucky? I didn't know. I wanted nothing more than this bag off my leg. I sipped my tea and started to choke. The nurse showed concerned and said, "Are you okay?"

"Yes," I lied. Like so many times before.

Shame. Worry. Doubt. Fear. My cohort from all of my life. Why don't I just speak up instead of having these damn little conversations in my head?

No, I wasn't okay. I was scared to death that I'd have to wear this ugly thing forever because my bladder wouldn't work right. The thought the purse would be there when I wanted to make love to my husband haunted me. The thought of it being there when I slid on a beautiful, sexy negligee made me nauseous. I didn't find it sexy but I knew Paul would take me anyway he could have me. I was my own worst critic. I'll probably never wear it again, or sexy underwear! I felt like an old lady with it and it never stopped bothering me.

I was definitely being hard on myself but fear of the un-known or imagined negative knowns does strange things to a person. The yellow bag had been with me for eight long weeks, always with me, needing to be replaced, cleaned and changed. *Crap!!* I wanted freedom again, I deserved getting this thing off.

I didn't realize how lucky I'd been before without it. I just didn't know.

The tech helped me onto the big spinning wheel and strapped me in. There was a place for my feet to be strapped in as well. They confirmed with me that I finished a dye drink earlier and had a lot of water to make sure they could follow the die on the machine as I was twirled around on the wheel. I was nervous and I had to pee. *Great, they just buckled me in.*

As they turned the wheel from the control room, they took images of the inside of my bladder. The results would be very much like a CT scan.

The doctor was making notes as they placed my body upside down, head to the ground. I felt the blood rush to my head and got instantly hot. The feeling of having to pee dissipated.

Good juju, good magic, I thought over and over in my mind, seeking to manifest a positive outcome. Only good juju.

It took a good thirty minutes to get all the images they wanted, and I was turned upside down on the wheel a few times, dying to pee the whole while.

They were able to give me my results after the test was completed. "You are free to go Susan!" the incredibly young doctor said.

"What?" I said with the biggest question mark ever.

"Go down the hall, first door to your left, and the nurse will take off your Foley, the bladder bag on your leg. You don't need it anymore! It's all healed up and back to normal. There is no leakage." I'm pretty sure my mouth was wide open with happy surprise.

"Check with your doctor if you have any further questions, and the bathroom is by the office door on your left." He said it like it was any other day for him.

For me it wasn't just any other day. I felt so damn lucky! I won the grand prize with The Wheel of Fortune! *Thank you. Thank you, universe.*

I would no longer have to carry this urine bag with me every day, day in and day out. I was so lucky, so grateful for this very moment where I felt so damn jubilant and I can still feel that joy to this day! I hugged the doctor, and he seemed surprised.

"I'm so happy!" I said again. I made a mental note to contact Dr. Mitchell and let him know about my recovery, and to thank him again.

"Thank you so very much!! You have no idea how much it means to me to take that thing off! Thank you, thank you, thank you!" I said as I started walking out the door.

"You're welcome!" he said studying the piece of paper in his hand, most likely for the next patient.

I'm pretty sure I skipped like a little girl all the way down the hall, and later, all the way to my car.

Chapter Nineteen

2017, I'M FIFY-SIX

Four years passed effortlessly. Nevaeh's toddler years whizzed by so fast.

Paul and I had a special gift, the gift of being a parent and the gift of life in our daughter, Nevaeh. We were happy as a family of three. Extended family with the boys, Brian and Steven but they were now off on their own after college and our little girl was getting big fast.

I was in my office working on my first book when I heard my cell phone ring. I picked it up one day when Paul was a work. I was at home and just getting ready to go pick Nevaeh up at preschool. It was a gentleman from our IVF doctor's office in Irvine, California. After we said our hello's he stated the reason for his call.

"Do you plan on keeping your three frozen embryos frozen, or would you, and your husband, Paul, consider adopting them out to a couple in need?" he asked.

I stopped as I caught my breath, holding the phone steadily to my ear and putting down what I was working on. Suddenly, it was a pivotal moment, and everything else became secondary.

We needed to make a decision about our embryos! I'd never met this man I was talking to, but I could tell by his soft spoken and steady voice he knew it was a touchy, tender subject.

It had been almost five years since the birth of our daughter. Paul and I thought deeply and talked about the embryos on more than one occasion. At one point we thought seriously about hiring a surrogate and started the process until we decided that we were at a point in our lives where we felt our family was complete.

It was a real full circle moment then when I thought about the reality of hiring a surrogate mother. We got all the way to choosing a surrogate mother and then opting out at contract time when we realized that in fact, our family was complete.

I reflected on raising my second family, and Paul, his first. Could we, or would we do the whole baby thing again? We knew we didn't want to keep the embryos frozen forever.

"Yes," I said. My mind instantly tried to verify it really was me who said yes. "We are ready. I mean, we'd love to find a good and loving home for them." I knew I was speaking for Paul as well. After I hung up with the man from the IVF center, I thought about all the possibilities.

I thought about the three possible brothers or sisters our daughter might have, but we weren't moving in that direction. We weren't making it happen.

Nevaeh is the most amazing child at almost five years old. She has long crimson hair and light blue-green eyes made to light up your life the moment you speak to her. Everyone seems to love her the moment they meet her. She's the kind of child who was born a vegan (even though we are not) and wants to grow up to be a vet. Her energy is constant, her conversational ability nonstop, and her giggle is contagious. She possesses a unique, strong-willed stubborn streak that sent me running for advice in parenting books this second time around as a mom to a young child.

I remembered reading about frozen embryos within the last few years, and how people are unable to make decisions about them. Currently, the latest data reveals there are well over 620,000 frozen embryos across the country waiting for adults to make decisions. Peter, the guy from the IVF center told us our three choices for the frozen embryos.

1. Donate them to research.
2. Destroy them.
3. Let them be adopted to couples in need.

There actually is a 4th option but no one tells you about it. It is the one most people with leftover embryos use because it can often be a personal and difficult decision to make.

4. Keep them frozen indefinitely.

When we first started IVF six years ago, Paul and I swore we would not keep any frozen embryos longer than five years. By then we thought we would know whether or not we wanted more children. The time had come and we had to make a choice about the future of our three frozen 'maybe babies.'

Where did the time go?

I always felt compassionate toward my past intended mothers, but my experience has given me an entirely new perspective of what my intended mothers went through while I was their surrogate mother. Now I knew first-hand the true ugliness of infertility.

Paul and I started the process of embryo donation so another family would be able to adopt our embryos. The first thing was to draft a letter. We decided the first letter would be to our three future frozen embryos.

January, 2017

Dear Loved Ones,

We write this letter to all three of you with so much love in knowing you will have a chance at life.

If you are reading this letter, you're now at an age where you understand how you came to be in this world. You were brought together at a doctor's office because we wanted desperately to have a family together.

We met, fell in love and married later in life, Paul, your biological father, and Susan. We tried to get pregnant a few times with Susan's eggs first because the IVF doctor thought they had promise for a woman fifty years of age. We tried one egg at a time every month, and it was difficult and stressful. Mother Nature intervened, and then we knew it wasn't going to be this time or any other time with Susan's eggs. It would have required a lot more medication and a lot more time before it 'might' work and we knew there was a chance it might never work.

All we wanted was to become parents. Before we went the IVF route, we thought about adopting children who needed families, or via embryo adoption. We kept running up against closed pathways, and nothing was promising. Being that Susan knew a lot about IVF, we decided it might work for us. We dug deep and found the finances to support our decision.

With assistance from a healthy younger woman, we were lucky enough to get five quality embryos the first time. We wrote an open-ended agreement with our egg donor, your biological egg donor mother. She helped us have you and agreed to meet any children she helped come into the world. We chose her because she fit more into what our future plans looked like, and to have a chance to make her part of our lives. It was important to us that you have the choice to know where you came from.

We received a call from the doctor's office asking us if we'd thought about the status of our embryos. You.

We decided on an open-ended embryo adoption, which means you will always have the choice to know us, your full biological sister, our daughter Nevaeh, and your older step-brothers from Susan's prior marriage. It is our hope someone will adopt you who might be as open as we are, and someone who wants to be loving parents like we did. Not just because they don't have kids, but because they truly want to be parents.

The doctor's office informed us they had a list of people who would love to adopt you. There were couples that have been through it all, too, with nothing but heartache and disappointment in trying to start a family. This choice of ours gave your mother the chance to be pregnant. She would feel life grow inside of her and feel your first kick, which feels like the flutter of a hundred butterflies.

With our letting go, a family will be made.

We're planning to meet a few couples in person this summer, and will choose your new mother and father. It's a difficult and important decision, but one we will make with caution, care, and love.

We'll be there when the transfer of embryos takes place, and hopefully form a relationship like an extended family. The hard part about picking a couple is you can never demand that a couple you've just met fit into your family's life.

It's not certain any of us will become friends, but we're going to try. Life experience has shown us that you can know someone twenty plus years and never really know them, because life situations and people change. We'll do our best though because we only want the best for you.

We decided not to give you up, but to give you all a chance at life.

Love Always,
Susan and Paul

Chapter Twenty

Close to two more years have passed. I always wonder about time. Is time really here or there? Or is it only here to mark our human existence, nothing else.

Because I've been through a lot of IVF processes, surrogacy and so many other things that require a lot of planning, paperwork and extreme details, I've never run up against the seemingly easy system of embryo donation. Paul and I learned it is not an easy process. It comes with its own challenges with requirements, endless forms, letter writing, consents, lab tests, FDA regulations and quite frankly, I could see why there are still so many embryos frozen. The agency doesn't make the process easy, but we made it through. We went back to Dr. Yanagi's IVF office when they called to tell us they had several couples in mind that would love to be parents.

We made it to embryo donation and our little embryos will soon have a chance at life.

My path in life has been an interesting one. I don't know anyone with a past like mine, but I too have not walked in others' shoes.

Our lives are as individual as our fingerprints.

I would not change a thing because I've learned so much

and continue to learn. I have a small silver rectangle paper weight on my desk from Michelangelo that says, "I am still learning…" I hold it close and remember every day there is something new to learn.

Most importantly what I learned was what I thought would kill me – didn't.

It moved me into a new perspective, and onto new paths of understanding and maybe into a whole new future path of employment. I've been looking into working as a death doula. It is exactly as it sounds; you help a person who is dying transition into death openly and assist their family with death coping skills. I'm excited about venturing into it and helping those who might see death in a different light.

Death wasn't the end for me, it was just the beginning.

The beginning of looking hard and long at death, the possibility of seeing it differently than I ever have in the past. I found it's impossible to die and become nothing. If we are energy then we will transform that energy into something, maybe consciousness when we die. Maybe it's a life continuation, like a full circle.

It was also the beginning of endless questions I still ask myself every day while thinking about my NDE almost every day of my life since I've had it, almost seven years ago. I know there is more I need to do with this experience but getting this book done is just the start.

I believe with all my heart the purpose of my NDE has not only to awakened my consciousness but has given me a pathway, a framework to revisit whenever I want to. It was activated in a way science hasn't been able to measure.

It's all connected, we're all connected.

Could it be possible that perhaps the universe is a giant conscious living organism? Perhaps. A good hard fact to compare it to is that the characteristics of living organisms is birth, growth, reproduction and death. According to many researchers of the cosmos, these three things are also plausible for the universe. We know it expands which would be growth, and what about reproduction, does it reproduce itself into multiverses? The laws of nature are so perfectly tuned, and I believe universes can harbor life, just not the kind we are used to. If the energy changes, it can create something totally different, unique and unimagined.

After a half a century on the earth, I've learned most of the answers to the questions I've asked, pleaded for and begged for sometimes. They finally came to me. I found God had a sense of humor because the funniest thing of all was that the answers to all of it, everything I've ever need to learn was inside of me the whole time since the day I was born.

Every experience I've had throughout my life, whether it be a risk-taker or like a death wish, my center weight of gravity shifted, and the experience alone changed me. Every single time it happened, it allowed me to renew my vow to life, to live fully.

Perhaps living fully gives us purpose in our lives, and gives us hope for humanity.

About The Author

Susan Ring lives in Orange County, California with her daughter, Nevaeh and husband, Paul with two very interactive cats. Susan's two grown boys, Brian and Steven, reside in Los Angeles, CA.

If you would like to visit Susan, you can check out her new website at www.susanaring.com

Printed in Great Britain
by Amazon